3ω

D0287559

This
Is
HERMAN CAIN!

My Journey to the White House

Herman Cain

THRESHOLD EDITIONS

NEW YORK   LONDON   TORONTO   SYDNEY   NEW DELHI

Threshold Editions
A Division of Simon & Schuster, Inc.
1230 Avenue of the Americas
New York, NY 10020

First Threshold Editions hardcover edition October 2011

THRESHOLD EDITIONS and colophon are trademarks of
Simon & Schuster, Inc.

For information about special discounts for bulk purchases,
please contact Simon & Schuster Special Sales at 1-866-506-1949
or business@simonandschuster.com.

The Simon & Schuster Speakers Bureau can bring authors to
your live event. For more information or to book an event,
contact the Simon & Schuster Speakers Bureau at 1-866-248-3049
or visit our website at www.simonspeakers.com.

Designed by Akasha Archer

Manufactured in the United States of America

10   9   8   7   6   5

Library of Congress Cataloging-in-Publication Data

Cain, Herman.
   This is Herman Cain! : my journey to the White House / Herman Cain.
   p.   cm.
   1. Cain, Herman.   2. Cain, Herman—Political and social views.
3. Presidential candidates—United States—Biography.   4. Businessmen—
United States—Biography.   5. Presidents—United States—Election—2012.
I. Title.
   E901.1.C35A3 2011
   324.973—dc23
   [B]   2011033425

ISBN 978-1-4516-6613–7
ISBN 978-1-4516-6615-1 (ebook)

This book is dedicated to my mother and father,
Lenora and Luther;
to my wife, Gloria;
to my children, Melanie and Vincent;
and to my grandchildren, Celena, Preston, and Ryan.

ON MY JOURNEY NOW

On my journey now (Mount Zion),
On my journey now (Mount Zion),
Well I wouldn't take nothing (Mount Zion),
For my journey now (M-o-u-n-t Zion)

One day one day (Mount Zion),
I was walking along (Mount Zion),
And the elements opened (Mount Zion),
And love came down (M-o-u-n-t Zion)

You can talk about me (Mount Zion),
Just as much as you please (Mount Zion),
But I'll talk about you (Mount Zion)
When I get on my knees (M-o-u-n-t Zion)

—Traditional Negro spiritual,
as sung by the Morehouse College Glee Club (1963–67)

CONTENTS

Contents

THIS IS HERMAN CAIN!

I'm Running for President

They that trust in the LORD shall be as Mount Zion,
which cannot be moved but abideth forever.

—Psalm 125:1

My name is Herman Cain.

I didn't grow up wanting to be president of the United States. I grew up po', which is even worse than being poor.

My American dream entailed working hard and making $20,000 a year, but I surpassed that goal and became a corporate CEO, a regional chairman of the Federal Reserve, a president of the Restaurant Association, an author, and an Atlanta talk show host before retiring at sixty-five on cruise control. And then I became a presidential aspirant.

But a strange thing happened on my way to cruise control: The country got off-track. On the evening of January 22, 1999, as I held my first grandchild, Celena, in my arms only moments after her birth, I realized that I needed to turn off the cruise control and help make this nation a better place. I needed to help make it a place in which Celena and the generations to come after her would be able to realize their full human potential and fulfill their own American dreams.

So at 12:46 P.M. on Saturday, May 21, 2011, I walked onto a platform at Centennial Olympic Park, in my hometown, Atlanta, Georgia, wearing one of my favorite gold ties—gold is my power color—and waved to the crowd of fifteen thousand and told them what they had been waiting to hear (for over two hours in more than ninety-degree heat): "I'm running for president of the United States and I'm not running for second!"

Looking out into the crowd and spotting my eighty-one-year-old aunt, Bessie Randall, one of my mother's sisters, I told the crowd, "She hasn't decided if she can vote for me yet, but I'm going to change her mind, just like I'm going to change the minds of other Americans."

Twenty-five minutes later, having articulated my "Cain Doctrine" to the cheering, banner-waving crowd, without printed speech or teleprompter, because I don't do teleprompters—I like to say I'm a *leader*, not a reader—I recalled the words of the Reverend Dr. Martin Luther King, Jr., and declared that when all the votes are counted on Tuesday, November 6, 2012, "We will be free at last! Free at last! Thank God Almighty! This nation will be free at last—again!"

Then I got off that platform and went back to the green room, where I joined Gloria, my wife of nearly forty-three years; our children, Melanie and Vincent; and our three grandkids (and we have another on the way). And there, of course, was Aunt Bessie. Strolling over to where she was, I couldn't resist asking, "Well, Aunt Bessie, *now* are you going to vote for me?"

"I guess I'm going to," she said, as if resigned to her fate.

It had been a mere sixteen days since I had redefined campaign history during the first debate of candidates for the Republican Party's 2012 presidential nomination, at the Peace Center, in Greenville, South Carolina, on the evening of Thursday, May 5, 2011.

Just before I went out on that stage that night, Mark Block, my campaign's chief operating officer, gave me some of the best, most calming, advice I have ever gotten: He said, "Herman, you don't have to be perfect out there. Just be Herman Cain."

His words gave me a deeper level of confidence and I said to the audience, "I'm proud that I haven't held public office before! How does *that* work for you?"

It did.

Then, when asked to make my concluding statement, I declared: "We need leadership, not more position-ship. God bless America!"

When I walked off that stage, I didn't even consider if I had distinguished myself. I just thought: I didn't make any major mistakes. I just answered the questions as well as I could.

I went into the green room and looked up at the television monitor. There was pollster Frank Luntz, asking a focus group gleaned from the auditorium audience how many people had supported me before the debate. Only one person raised her hand. I thought: I guess this is not going to work. But then, Frank asked how many people supported me now, and suddenly I saw all these hands go up. And then I heard Frank say, "Just stop right there!" Those words are going to be ringing in my ears for the rest of my life.

I was as surprised as everybody else. That debate was the

game changer and my candidacy took off like a rocket. We knew that my name identification and my inclusion in the polls was going to take some time, so we developed a from-the-ground-up strategy of getting out to know the people.

But what, everyone wondered, made the audience respond the way it did?

Maybe it's that I've always been a no-nonsense person. Maybe my straight-from-the-heart approach struck a resonant chord. But those participants in Frank Luntz's focus group voted me the debate's winner, as did 49 percent of viewers on the Fox News Channel. The closest runner-up was Ron Paul—and he only had 25 percent of the vote!

So how did I, the debate participant who mounted the platform as a relative political unknown, manage to capture the hearts and minds of thousands of American voters—and manage to do it in ninety minutes?

How did I, a proud "outsider," go on to outdistance four better-known presidential aspirants—Tim Pawlenty, Gary Johnson, Ron Paul, and Rick Santorum—in a Gallup Poll conducted between May 20 and 24, 2011?

And how did I manage to place just behind front runners Mitt Romney and Sarah Palin in a Quinnipiac University Poll released on June 8?

This is Herman Cain.

· · · · · · · · ·

The second debate took place from eight to ten o' clock on the evening of Monday, June 13, at the Sullivan Arena on the campus of Saint Anselm College, in Manchester, New Hampshire. It was jointly sponsored by the *New Hampshire Union Leader*, local television station WMUR, and CNN, and broadcast by that cable channel.

Now, I had done political debates when I ran for the U.S. Senate in 2004, against two Georgia congressmen. Those debates were no contest, but this was a *presidential* debate, and people's expectations were different.

So while I was a little nervous in New Hampshire, I was confident that I could hold my own because I was getting comments from people, like on the afternoon before the debate, when we stopped in at Sal's Pizza Place for an informal visit.

People came up to me and said, "You know what I like most about what you said in that last debate? When you said you don't have all the information—that you didn't pretend you have a plan for Afghanistan."

Comments like that confirmed what Mark Block had told me before I walked out onto that platform in South Carolina: "Just be Herman Cain." That was the same feeling I had as I strolled out onto the platform at Saint Anselm College.

Did I study for that debate? Yes. Did I do "debate prep" with my staff? Yes. Those guys put me through it from two to four on the Friday afternoon before the debate—we just talked about issues and content. The next morning, we did about four more hours. Then we had lunch and just kept on talking about the topics, so, actually, I had about seven hours with my debate team. And they were *intense*.

Did I study a lot of material? Yes, of course I did; I had a complete transcript of the 2007 CNN debate, moderated by Wolf Blitzer, and I read the whole thing to get a feel for how they do debates. But you can overdo the prep and leave the fight in the gym.

So I had a decent night's sleep and left early Sunday morning for New Hampshire with my key staff. We did two events that afternoon: First I spoke at a Republican-sponsored picnic, which was fun, although some of the attendees were still trying to define their support, and then our drop-in at Sal's. I really enjoyed that one because it wasn't a Republican event: The people there were already supporters and they were there for *Herman Cain*. I didn't toss any pizza dough there, but it was great fun just interacting with the people. What encouraged me was that people who have never been politically minded are now getting involved—because they believe in us. You had people from Maine and Massachusetts there—a lady and her daughter drove 120 miles for twenty minutes of time with me. That kind of stuff tells you that something out of the ordinary is going on.

The political establishment doesn't *get* it and I'm fine with that. To be honest with you, I hope that they continue to *not* get it. But you can be sure they'll get it in January 2013 when I'm taking the oath of office as president!

On Monday, debate day, I was feeling confident. I began the morning by driving over to the arena with my key staff members for a "walk-through." Along the way, I relaxed by vocalizing and sang one of my favorite hymns, "To God Be the Glory." I've enjoyed singing for pleasure all my life, in my church's youth choir and as an adult performing once with the

Omaha Symphony Orchestra—that one was hard, but I practiced and practiced and pulled it off. That morning, when I followed up the hymn with the national anthem, one of the riders in the car said, "You could sing the 'Star Spangled Banner' at your own inauguration!"

Then somebody suggested that I sing it at the debate! I said, "If I did, Mark Block would have a heart attack."

"No," Mark said, "you'd get a standing ovation!"

"Well, if I did sing 'The Star Spangled Banner' at the debate," I answered, "at least no one would interrupt me!" And I thought: I might do that at a future debate, just to give the other candidates a fighting chance tonight. As my dad used to say, "Don't show out too early."

After the walk-through, I did one media event, a radio interview with an Atlanta-based talk radio colleague, Neal Boortz. I don't mind being on the radio with him because I feel close to him. And besides, I had all afternoon to rest, and, in fact, after enjoying lunch with my staff, I went back to our hotel for some "down time."

That evening, I was the first of the seven debate participants to walk onto the platform, the order having been determined by lottery. As I took my place at the far end of that platform, I made a mental vow: I'm going to be *myself*. Remember, I don't do canned responses. I believe people can smell them a mile away. I'm spontaneous. I'm who *I* am.

For the next two hours, during the rare moments when the moderator, John King, gave me the opportunity to weigh in, I spoke of my concerns about our nation's economic crisis.

The audience and viewers did not get the chance to learn

very much about how I plan to get America's economy back on the right track, but they did find out one important thing about the former CEO of Godfather's Pizza. During a lighter moment Mr. King asked whether I prefer deep dish to thin crust pizza, and I announced, in no uncertain terms, "Deep dish!"

I had walked onto that platform as the only one of the contenders for the Republican Party's 2012 presidential nomination to have run several companies; to have rescued one of them from the very brink of bankruptcy; and the only one to have during my career provided jobs for thousands of Americans seeking dignity and fulfillment of their American dreams.

That night, I slept like two rocks at the bottom of a pond.

Two days later, when I picked up my copy of *USA Today*, I read twenty-eight of the sweetest words written about me in the aftermath of my CNN appearance: "Cain, former CEO of Godfather's Pizza, topped the list of GOP hopefuls being searched through Yahoo during the debate and its immediate aftermath, according to the company's statistics."

That is Herman Cain.

· · · · · · · · ·

So what is it about *me* that prompted one out of every four people searching Yahoo's site to click on the name *Herman Cain* in those four hours between eight o'clock and midnight on the evening of the New Hampshire debate?

What is it in my DNA that years ago prompted me to take

on the enormous challenge of doing my part toward making America a better place for Celena and the generations to come?

Why do I, a son of the segregated South, refuse to think of myself as a "victim" of racism?

What is it that motivates me to insist on defining my identity in terms of "ABC"—as being American first, black second, and conservative third—as I did to cheers from the crowd in Atlanta on May 21?

Just who *is* Herman Cain?

And how did I get *this way*?

Just a hint: It may have something to do with lessons learned from my parents, Lenora and Luther Cain, Jr.

Welcome to *This Is Herman Cain!*

Growing Up Poor
in the Segregated South

We are troubled on every side, yet not distressed;
We are perplexed, but not in despair;
persecuted, but not forsaken;
cast down, but not destroyed . . .

—2 Corinthians 4:8–9

One day in 1943, Dad, who was eighteen years old at the time, walked off my grandparents' farm in rural Arlington, Tennessee, with only the clothes he was wearing. But, in fact, he was blessed with more valuable possessions—his faith in God, his self-confidence, and his belief in the American dream.

He walked and hitchhiked all the way to Mansfield, Ohio—I never knew why he went *there*—and found work in a tire-manufacturing plant. He was determined to earn enough money to build a better life than his father had been able to do, having struggled constantly merely to earn enough to provide the barest of essentials for my grandmother and their twelve children, all of them crammed into a three-room house.

At around that time, Mom, born Lenora Davis, also eighteen and also, like my dad, seeking a better life, walked off her parents' farm in Douglasville, Georgia, about thirty minutes' drive west of Atlanta, and made her way to Ohio, where she went to stay with an aunt living in Mansfield.

One of Mom's cousins found her a job as a maid. In order to get to her workplace, Mom had to ride with her cousin. They in turn would be picked up by her cousin's boyfriend, in his truck, on *his* way to work. The truck had one of those cabs where you could only sit three people in the front. One morning, when the cousin's boyfriend showed up, another guy was already sitting in the cab. As there was only room for three people to sit there, Mom had a choice: either sit in Luther Cain's lap or not go to work. She needed to go to work, so she sat in Luther Cain's lap. He was thrilled. After all, Lenora Davis was a good-looking young woman. They did this for several weeks. They started dating. About a year later, he popped the question.

Lenora Davis and Luther Cain, Jr., were married in Ohio. They moved back to Memphis for a short period of time, and I was born there on December 13, 1945. My brother Thurman came along eighteen months later, and we soon moved to Atlanta, because Mom's folks were from Stone Mountain, in the greater metropolitan area. Mom was homesick and moving there made her happy. Besides, Atlanta was a much more promising city than Memphis for job opportunities, and Dad was going to find other work, which he did.

Dad was not only the head of our family, but also the head of our extended family. Many of his friends sought his great common sense advice or came to him when they were down on their luck, or in trouble. He had a natural, motivating, competitive spirit, and even though he sometimes thought he was "the only man in the arena," he always had compassion for other people.

He became a deacon in our church and it was not long before he was asked to become chairman of the Deacon Board. Then he joined the choir—possessing a natural gift of stage presence, he became a lead singer—and it was not long before he ended up being its president.

My dad was also a big-time Brooklyn Dodgers fan. When they brought Jackie Robinson on, many baseball fans in America became instant Brooklyn Dodgers fans. Then when they moved to LA, my dad was heartbroken. It wasn't the same because even though the Dodgers had national appeal, they were from Brooklyn, and they were losing their identity.

My very first memories were of when my brother and I were little boys—Thurman must have been about four; I was five—and we were living in an apartment at the end of a building in what we called "the Projects," government-supported housing downtown, on Gray Street, not two hundred yards from where the Convention Center now stands.

I can remember attending Gray Street Elementary School, up the street from the Projects. One day, our teacher told us,

"You're not getting the same education as white students." When she said that, I really didn't get mad. I just decided: Okay, I know that, but I'm still going to work as hard as I can to succeed, despite the fact that the white kids have better materials and better books.

My attitude then—as it is to this very day—was that you take a seemingly impossible goal and you *make* it happen. That was one of the many lessons I learned from Dad: He never allowed his lack of formal education to be a barrier to his success. And he never allowed his starting point in life or the racial conditions of his time to be excuses for failing to pursue his dreams. Dad taught me the value of having dreams, the motivation to pursue them, and the determination to achieve them.

That value made it possible for me to contemplate running for president. Some people don't think I can get elected; they don't think I can be an effective president. But as my wife, Gloria, will tell you, "The first thing you do in order to inspire Herman to do something is just to tell him 'You can't do it.' Then, get out of his way!"

I gave my first speech at our church. I was eight years old and I can still recall my first words: "I wish my parents would stop talking about who I look like." I lost my first election in the seventh grade. It was for class president. Five years later, as a high school senior, I ran a second time, having been urged to do so by some of my classmates who recognized leadership qualities in me before I did.

There is a latter-day parallel of sorts: In 2004, I ran in Georgia for a Senate seat but lost that election. Now, seven years later, I'm out there campaigning for the Republican Party's presidential nomination! There's a message in that time-frame between defeat and success!

· · · · · · · · ·

It wasn't easy to raise a family in the segregated Atlanta of the 1950s and 1960s. Dad wanted a nice house and a nice car and to put away enough savings to provide for Mom in the event of his death. But, above all, he wanted to put Thurman and me through college.

I'll never forget the day when I was in fourth grade that we moved from the Projects to our house on Pelham Street, three rooms of a six-room duplex I called "the half-a-house." Life was hard, but decidedly better there than before. To make ends meet and still have the hope of making a better life for Thurman and me, Mom worked as a maid and Dad worked three jobs: as a barber, as a janitor at the Pillsbury Company, and as a chauffeur at the Coca-Cola Company.

Dad worked all three jobs until he could make it off of two jobs; then he worked those two jobs until he could make it off of that one job. That was a typical experience shared by many Americans.

Mom and Dad were able to achieve their dreams because we didn't have government in the way as much as it is in the way today. And Dad was so well thought of at Coca-Cola that he eventually became the private chauffeur to Robert W. Woodruff, the corporation's chairman and CEO. Dad's job was demanding, being on call whenever Mr. Woodruff was in town, but he was not required to accompany his boss on out-of-town trips, so he was able to spend time with us, to guide us, and to offer us glimpses of corporate life.

I relished those moments. While we were financially poor, we were emotionally rich, and our hard-working parents taught us lessons in dignity, ambition, and the value of formal education. Dad didn't have the opportunity to earn a college degree, but I always tell people that he had a Ph.D. in common sense, and that he had graduated with honors—*cum laude.*

Dad developed much of his philosophy of life and learned a lot working for Mr. Woodruff, who was an inspiring personality. He was a good businessman, a risk-taker, and very benevolent. And he had a big heart. He cared about the city, so the Coca-Cola Corporation contributed a lot of money to the Atlanta University Center, which includes Morehouse College. Mr. Woodruff also created the center's Woodruff Library, and Atlanta's Woodruff Arts Center was named for him. Coca-Cola also contributed to Georgia Tech, Emory, and every other major school in Atlanta.

R. W. Woodruff was also a champion of rights for blacks. Dad told me about the day in 1961 when two young, academically qualified students, Hamilton Holmes and Charlayne Hunter, both of whom had been screened and hand-picked, were attempting to enroll at the University of Georgia, but were being prevented by the school's president from doing so.

Coca-Cola was probably the largest corporation in Atlanta at that time because they were international, so they had a lot of clout in the state of Georgia. So R. W. Woodruff picked up the phone—he used to have a big cigar in his mouth and Dad imitated the way he talked—and told the president of the university, "We aren't having that here in Georgia. We're not going to make fools of ourselves like George Wallace did down in Alabama." He then called the governor and said, "Why are you going to fight letting them in? You don't have to. Why look stupid?"

R. W. Woodruff knew how devoted Dad was to him, and he loved and trusted Dad more than he trusted some of his executives, like Joe Jones, a white man, who handled his finances.

Mr. Woodruff was also very generous with gifts of cash. One day, Dad said to Woodruff, "I really like the gifts you've bought for me and I appreciate the cash, but, you know, I would also appreciate some Coca-Cola stock, if you wanted to give that to me."

So Woodruff started giving my dad stock, and he was generous with that, too. One day he told my dad, "Joe Jones doesn't think I ought to be giving you any stock, but I told him I was going to give it to you anyway." To Joe Jones, Woodruff's money was *his* money.

One day Dad said to Jones, "Mr. Jones, I'd like to see you outside for a minute." They walked out to the driveway and Dad said, "Do you see this gun I'm carrying?"—Dad had a permit to carry one because he was with Woodruff—"Do you know how good I can shoot this gun?"

"No," Joe Jones replied.

"I can throw a silver dollar up in the air and hit it four times before it hits the ground. That's how good a shot I am," my dad said. "If you ever tell Mr. Woodruff not to do something for me again, you're going to find out how good I am with this gun!"

He was joking, but my dad was unafraid: Nobody was going to mess with Luther Cain. Mr. Woodruff really respected him because my dad had innate self-determination. I have that same innate self-determination in my genes and I got it from Dad.

One of the most important lessons Dad taught us was not to feel like victims. He never felt like a victim; he never talked like a victim; he never expressed one "victim" attitude the whole while I knew him. It was his inner self-determination. He just never had that attitude, so *we* didn't have that attitude.

And both of our parents taught us not to think that the government owed us something. They didn't teach us to be mad at this country. They would always say to us: "If you want something, just work hard enough, focus on it, and guess what? You can make it *happen!*"

And Dad made things happen. One day in the summer before I started the eighth grade, he came home and said to us: "Get in the car; we're going for a ride." He drove us to a suburb west of Atlanta, pulled up in front of a six-room, all-brick house on Albert Street, and said, "This is our new home." He had fulfilled his dream of being able to buy a "whole house."

Dad had a winning attitude about everything he did, no matter what. One day, when Thurman and I were teenagers, we were outside with Dad, just kidding around, and I don't know how it came up, but Dad said, "I can still outrun you all!"

Being that Dad was kind of overweight, I said, "No, you can't!"

"Yes, I *can*," he insisted, "I can *outrun* you!"

So Dad challenged us, two young teenagers, to a foot race, right in the middle of Albert Street. There wasn't a lot of traffic and he was just having fun, so we said, "Okay, Dad."

We knew we could outrun my dad but we went out into the middle of the street. Then just before we started the race he said, "Now, you all have got to move back a hundred yards and give me a head start!"

"That wasn't part of the deal!" we said.

"*Move back!*" he said.

And we *did*. I don't even remember the result of that race. It was just so much fun—my brother and I running as fast as we could and my dad just chugging up the street.

Dad may or may not have been able to outrun us, but he had an amazing ability to think on his feet. I'll never forget the time, many years after that foot race, that by doing so, he got himself out of a jam.

Having walked off my grandparents' farm when he was eighteen, Dad's material American dream was to own a Cadillac, the dream car for somebody who had nothing. His family couldn't afford a car and Dad had never owned one before. So after working three jobs, Dad bought his first one, a black one, and he achieved that American dream.

He kept that car for a while and then he wanted to buy a new one. So he bought a white Cadillac that had all of these extra chrome fixtures on it, including a chrome horse on the front of the hood. That was the era of chrome; today you would call it a drug dealer's car—you get the image?

He was proud of that car, with all the chrome—I remember

thinking it was ostentatious—and he sold me the black one at a very attractive price, so I took it, because we were living in Virginia and we had a lot of driving back and forth to come home, and it was nice to have a comfortable Cadillac to ride in.

Then three or four years later, he decided he wanted to get another car—remember, this was a man who had started with *nothing*—and because they didn't have Lexuses or BMWs then, he wanted another Cadillac, and he wanted me to buy the white Cadillac. I said okay and he bought a dark green one, so I asked, "What are you going to do with the black Cadillac?" He said he was going to give it to *his* father, who was about eighty years old, and was living on the farm in Tennessee.

My dad's sister had died and we were going to Tennessee for the funeral. As I had bought the white Cadillac, and Dad had to bring the green Cadillac up for the funeral, we ended up having to drive three Cadillacs. On the way from Atlanta to Memphis, you have to go through Alabama and Mississippi, and not much of Arkansas, and then you get into Tennessee. So we're driving in the South, in a caravan of three Cadillacs, with three black drivers—I was driving the white one, Thurman was driving the black one, and my dad was driving his new green one.

We all had CB radios, so were staying in touch with one another—I love cornbread, so that was my handle—and we were communicating with truckers who were telling us where the police were. We were driving eighty-five miles an hour in those three Cadillacs—and every once in a while, I'd go: "This is Cornbread, 10–4 on Smokey and the Bandit."

Then a trucker would come back with, "Ten-four, Corn-bread, when you get to about mile-marker 89, you're going to see a couple of police on your left, going in the opposite direction, so you may want to slow down."

"Ten-four, this is Cornbread. Thank you very much."

My cousin Jeanine—she was a little younger than I am—was riding with us and she said, "Let me talk on that thing." Well, she kept on talking to Dad and Thurman, "Breaker, Breaker, 19–50, Bunny Rabbit . . . "

I said, "What kind of handle is *'Bunny Rabbit'*?"

"You need a different handle," Thurman told her.

Well, they were just chit-chatting, so we couldn't hear the truck drivers who were telling us, "You've got the cops just around the corner."

Lo and behold, when Bunny Rabbit got off chit-chatting, we went around this corner and there was a cop standing there with a radar gun. He caught us coming around that corner at ninety miles an hour. I was in the front because Thurman had said, "I'm going to keep up with you," and Dad was in the third car.

The cop started motioning for us to pull over and we did. Dad got out and Thurman got out, and the cop said, "You boys were going pretty fast. We've got you clocked at about eighty-nine miles an hour and we've got to write you up a ticket. Why are you all in such a hurry?"

Dad said, "We're headed up for my sister's funeral, and we were just trying to get there," which was true.

And the cop said, "Well, I'll have to write you up because you're all going way too fast over the speed limit."

So, Dad, who has that Ph.D. in common sense, said to the cop, "Officer, how many cars can you clock at one time?"

And he said, "Just one."

Dad said, "So you clocked the front car?"

"Yep," the cop said.

"So you really didn't clock the second two?"

"You know, you're right," the cop said. "Since you're going to a funeral, I'm just going to write a ticket for the one in front."

That was *me*. Imagine my dad thinking that quickly on his feet! The cop wrote one ticket, and he wrote it to *me*.

Then, when we get back on the road, one of the truckers came on and said, "Cornbread, how'd you all come out?"

"They stopped us," I told him.

Then *he* said, "We were trying to give you a warning, but somebody named Bunny Rabbit was on the CB."

When we got to Tennessee, Dad just laughed and laughed—he thought it was the funniest thing—and I said, "Daddy, *you* didn't have to pay the ticket."

And he said, "No. *You* got a ticket for speeding; *I* didn't."

My dad left that black Cadillac for *his* dad, for him to enjoy in his final years on Earth, and Dad asked him "Well, what do you think?"

And my granddad said—his nickname was "Papa Luke" and he was a very quiet, humble man—"That's nice." He didn't get overexcited, but you can imagine, when he drove to the little country church back in the woods, that he was as proud as he could be to be driving the black Cadillac that his son had given him.

Incidentally, my handle seems to be sticking to me. One member of my campaign staff, a young man named Nathan Naidu, insists that when I'm president my Secret Service name is going to be "Cornbread!" And in the meantime, he says, whenever he puts anything on my campaign schedule, instead of writing, "Mr. Cain," I'll be referred to as "Cornbread." Well thanks, Nate. You've just told the whole world my future Secret Service nickname!

Dad never spent much time looking at his life in the rearview mirror. He just kept moving ahead despite the many detours he encountered. Now, as I travel life's journey and some things grow dimmer and dimmer in my rearview mirror, Dad's inspiration becomes brighter and brighter. I often think of him and Mom as I'm about to deliver a speech. I think of the life lessons they taught that have brought me to this place, and I'm as proud of them as they were proud of me.

My dad was full of life. He loved being around people and loved having fun and loved to laugh. My mother used to say to me, "The older you get, the more you act just like your daddy."

I'd say, "Thanks, Mom. That's a compliment."

· · · · · · · · · ·

My childhood summers were spent on my maternal grandparents' farm. Mom had eight brothers and sisters, and they all would dump their kids on the grandparents, to give our parents a break, I guess. Maybe they were hoping that our grandparents would keep us indefinitely, but they wouldn't. So we'd have twenty to twenty-five kids staying with the grandparents.

When all of the grandkids were there at the same time, it seemed like it was dozens.

My grandparents were farmers all their lives—my grandmother lived to be 104 and my grandfather was 94 when he passed on. They grew all of the staples—watermelon, cantaloupe, corn, beans, tomatoes, potatoes, collard greens, and cabbage—and I remember my grandfather taking them into town, to the farmers' market, to sell them. He didn't do that a lot; he'd go sell to the people who were going to stay at the farmers' market, so he was like a wholesaler.

And my grandparents were very devout, churchgoing people. So even when I went to visit with them, I couldn't get away from the expectations that I had at home: You're going to church! It wasn't optional.

Back in Atlanta, notwithstanding the usual sibling disagreements, Thurman and I got along well, enjoying all manner of adventures. Thurman loved to laugh and to make other people laugh. But sometimes his idea of a good laugh got us both in trouble. One Christmas, when I was ten and he was nine, our parents bought us BB guns as presents. We took the guns over to an aunt's house and were playing outdoors when Thurman pointed his gun at our older cousin, Elizabeth. He told her not to move but she did move after daring him to shoot, so he shot her in the butt. Elizabeth was not really hurt but that BB did sting. Needless to say, Mom took the guns away from us and we never saw them again.

One very hot day when he and I were out with Mom, we got very thirsty and started to walk over to a public water fountain. Mom reminded us that we must use the "coloreds" fountain. Being somewhat rambunctious, however, we made sure no one was watching us, and then we drank, first from the forbidden "whites only" fountain, and after that from the "coloreds" fountain. Then we looked at each other and said, "You know what? The 'whites only' water tastes just the same as the 'coloreds' does!"

On a day-to-day basis, because the civil rights movement was a few years in front of me, I was too young to participate when they first started the Freedom Rides, and the sit-ins. So on a day-to-day basis, it didn't have an impact. I just kept going to school, doing what I was supposed to do, and stayed out of trouble—I didn't go downtown and try to participate in sit-ins.

But I well remember, as a young teenager, seeing signs printed in large black letters at the fronts of buses: "White seat from front, colored seat from rear." One day when I was thirteen, my friends and I were riding home from school in a half-empty bus—this was at the time when the civil rights movement was just getting off the ground and some police officers were just looking for a reason to shoot a black person who "got out of line." So, counter to our real feelings, we decided to avoid trouble by moving to the back of the bus when the driver told us to.

By that time, the sit-ins and the Freedom Rides had kind of broken the ice, even though things hadn't fully changed. So we saw it every day on TV and read about it in the news. Dad always said, "Stay out of trouble," and we did.

· · · · · · · · ·

At Archer High School, my role models were my mathematics teacher, Charles Johnson, and our band director, Lloyd Terry. I never thought of myself as having an aptitude in mathematics, or of being some sort of mathematical prodigy, but I always did well in that subject. I made A's all the way through high school, and I thought maybe the rest of the students in my math class were just dumber than I was.

One of the reasons I did well in that subject was that I had a great mathematics teacher in Mr. Johnson. He didn't focus on teaching us the more complex concepts. He focused instead on making sure we understood the simple concepts. As he explained to us: "If you understand the simple concepts, you will be able to deal with the complex concepts."

So if he had to take two days on a particular subject in order to satisfy some requirement, he would take two days to do it. And he wasn't under any pressure, like teachers are today, to finish a certain curriculum in a given amount of time. He wanted to make sure that we learned what we *needed* to learn in those early concepts, even if we didn't get into the more complicated stuff.

Mr. Johnson was also unique as a teacher in that on some Fridays when we came into class, he wouldn't even teach math; he would sit down and just talk to us about what was going on in our lives, or what was going on in the world. He would ask us, "Do you all know what the president has done, and why?"

He would talk to us that way for *the whole hour* because he knew we were not getting that at home—most of the kids were from the kind of background I came from: My parents were so busy working and just trying to live that they didn't have time to sit down and chit-chat about current events. Mr. Johnson was cut from a mold that hardly exists today.

It was at around that time that I began to develop my concept of being responsible for one's success or failure in life—a concept I would later come to define as being a "CEO of Self"—a time when many of the qualities of determination and leadership that I inherited from my dad began to show up.

As my first goal had been to find a job that paid $20,000 a year, I realized that I had to take charge of my life, to distinguish the difference between having a dream and working toward achieving a goal—in other words, to become my own chief executive of self. A goal is something you can quantify. It is the path to your dream. The thing that connects your current goal and your next goal to your dream is called faith—faith in yourself and in your God. And you don't whisper your goal to yourself. You say it out loud so that all your senses can participate in the process. It is important to recognize that not everybody's dream or goal is going to be achieved on a fast track, or in a straight line. Your job is to continuously prepare yourself for whatever opportunities come along.

There are three steps involved in becoming a true CEO of Self. I call them ROI.

R: Remove barriers that prevent self-motivation to achieve goals.

O: Obtain the right results by working on the right problems.

I: Inspiration. Learn to inspire yourself.

In my experience, great leaders inspire others. But, more importantly, they inspire themselves.

During those years, Thurman and I shared several interests. We were musically inclined, both of us singing in our church's youth choir. I inherited Dad's vocal talent, and was asked to sing solo parts, as Dad had once done, while Thurman took after our mother, whose talents were more modest. I loved her dearly, but she couldn't carry a tune.

Thurman and I also played the trombone, becoming first chair in our respective high school and college bands. I joined my high school band in the eighth grade even though I had never played an instrument. When Mr. Terry asked me what instrument I wanted to learn, I replied, "What you need most." Even then, it wasn't about *me*.

He said that he was short of trombone players, so I learned to play the trombone. And by the time I reached tenth grade I was the leader of the trombone section. A year later, I was chosen to be the band's student director—the very first time a junior had been picked for that important position.

Mr. Terry taught all of us the meaning of what he called "the thrill of victory," which, he said, could be achieved through hard work, discipline, practice, and inner pride. He insisted that we could outplay any band in the state of Georgia if we willed ourselves to do so—an important lesson for me about the collective success of a group.

Our band leader's encouragement helped me to summon the pride, motivation, and confidence already inside me to flourish and grow. After all, just as a seed of corn needs fertile soil, water, and sunshine to grow to its plentiful harvest, success starts inside and must be cultivated with encouragement and accomplishment to prevent the growth of "weeds" of doubt.

Thurman graduated from Morris Brown College and then started his career as a computer programmer with Shell Oil in Houston. A few years later he came back to Atlanta to work at Coca-Cola. When his career as a programmer hit some detours he tried but did not succeed in several entrepreneurial ventures. But despite problems and disappointments exacerbated by alcohol and drug abuse, he never lost his love of living or his love of people.

I will always remember Thurman for the pride he took in his three daughters, and for some of the better choices he made in his all-too-short life. One major choice was his decision to remain in Atlanta so that he could help Dad when his health declined as a result of complications from diabetes. Thurman was the one who took Dad to the hospital for kidney dialysis treatments, and he chose to be at Mom's side when she began to suffer from the effects of multiple sclerosis.

I will forever be grateful to Thurman for being there for Mom and Dad when they needed him most.

Thurman died young, in 1999 at the age of fifty-two, because he made some choices that ruined his health and shortened his life, involving alcohol and drugs. I loved my brother dearly and still grieve over his untimely death. And I know that he is looking down proudly on my incredible journey.

— 2 —

CEO of Self

In quietness and confidence shall be thy strength.

—Isaiah 30:15

M om and Dad had always encouraged me to "be something." But they never told me *what* to be. When I was
still in high school, I thought that I would be a preacher or a
teacher—the only two white-collar professions to which I had
been exposed. But having been inspired by my father and my
math teacher, Mr. Johnson, to dream big dreams, I began to
see greater opportunities in my future.

Having been salutatorian of my high school class, as well as
president of the senior class, I received scholarship offers from
several historically black colleges. They didn't stem from my
standardized test scores, which were mediocre, largely because
I had poor reading habits growing up. While Mom and Dad
were loving and supportive, they never encouraged Thurman
and me to read books outside of the ones we had to read for

school. Nor did they read to us; they just didn't have time to do so.

I chose Morehouse College because of its location in Atlanta, which meant that I could commute by bus from home. When I enrolled there I had no idea of its great reputation as an institution of higher learning.

I was awarded a first-year tuition scholarship, which I lost because I couldn't maintain a B average. While I was disappointed, I didn't feel defeated, because I knew I had worked as hard as I could—that this was a mere speed bump on my way to realizing what I later called my "CEO of Self" goals.

I discovered just how competitive Morehouse was. Even though I had graduated as salutatorian, at Archer High School, that didn't mean anything. Everyone was a salutatorian. Big deal! My class actually had nine hundred valedictorians and salutatorians from all over the country.

The problem was being able to pay my tuition. Mom and Dad wanted me to continue my education and they helped out. But I had to work various part-time jobs during the school year and in the summers.

I was able to get a job working for an apartment complex where they hired kids to work for the summer. They were tearing up the basement of one of these buildings and we had to tear out all the concrete in the basement of this apartment building. I don't even know how I got the job— somebody must have told me: Go over there; they're looking for somebody.

There were all of these older construction guys working on this project, and the first thing they said to me the first day was, "This is how you do the jackhammer." They put me on that jackhammer and made me tear up concrete all day on that thing. I know they gave me the hardest job on purpose. When I went home that night, I was so tired that I could hardly eat dinner. My whole body was shaking from the noise. My mom said, "Are you going back tomorrow?"

I was *not* going to let that jackhammer defeat me. I was determined that the jackhammer was not going to be in my future. I said, "Yes, they're not going to make *me* quit." And I went back the next day. And because I showed up, they took me off the jackhammer.

They were *testing* me! Not long after that, my dad said, "They're looking for a summer assistant to work in the R&D lab over at Coca-Cola," and I was able to go and work in the R&D lab as an assistant for the rest of that summer—in an *air-conditioned* laboratory.

I could have dropped out of college, of course, but being CEO of Self, I had to stay and focus on whatever it took to get my degree, and I was fortunate to have the support of caring people who taught me to believe in God, to believe in myself, and to believe that I could accomplish anything I set my sights on accomplishing.

I thought when I was in Mr. Johnson's mathematics class at Archer High that I was a good math student. When I got to Morehouse, however, I found out that I was way behind some of those other guys. But Mr. Johnson said, "Major in math; you've got the ability to do that."

Majoring in math was the hardest thing I ever did. That's when I started learning a lot of these complex concepts that some of my classmates had learned in high school. So I simply *outworked* them—not to beat them, just to keep up. As for my reading problem, that began to be solved when I was required to take a semester-long remedial course.

Toward the end of my sophomore year, I came down with the measles and was out of school for a week, but I worked even harder to keep up. While my measles were not contagious by the time I took most of my final exams, I showed up for them with a pullover pulled up over my head because I still had all the measles bumps all over my face.

Then, during my senior year, I was given quite an honor: I was asked to join the Morehouse Quartet, due in part to the fact that I had previously been picked for the Glee Club, a very prestigious group, on my first attempt to join it. After that, I was elected, by secret ballot, its president. Again, it was evident that other people perceived my leadership potential even before I did.

I graduated from Morehouse with a B average in mathematics. The rest of my grade point average was C. but I maintained that B average in my major. I worked hard to get that degree. I *had* to.

The graduation ceremony was held at the Samuel Howard Archer auditorium (Archer was also the name of my high school) on the Morehouse campus. Dr. Benjamin E. Mays, the president of Morehouse, was the commencement speaker. He retired that year and was later elected to the Atlanta school board, where he served into his eighties.

I can still see Dad, who worked such long hours that he hadn't been able to attend most of the events I had participated in at Morehouse, sitting there, as proud as could be. Afterward, to celebrate, he took us out to dinner, not to the finest restaurant in Atlanta, but to the city's finest *soul food* restaurant, Paschals, known for its fried chicken, where he treated the family to a fried chicken dinner.

Just as my high school teachers had been my early role models, Benjamin Mays took a great interest in the students. He was a great man, a great leader, and a great educator who started out in very humble circumstances—he often talked to us about the town he grew up in. It was so small that it didn't even have a name and was simply called "96 South Carolina." He was like the "dad" of the campus. If a man got out of line, say at a football game, he would hear about it in chapel on Monday morning. It was the kind of tongue-lashing you didn't want to get.

Before deciding to attend Morehouse, I had also applied to the University of Georgia, as well as to the Georgia Institute of Technology—Georgia Tech—and I was not really surprised when those two state-funded schools denied me admission. Having been desegregated for only two years, they chose to keep enrollment of black students to a minimum.

Years later our daughter Melanie, although then living with us in Nebraska, was determined to attend the University of Georgia. I suspect her decision had something to do with an option I had not enjoyed. Melanie went on to graduate from the university in 1994.

My decision to attend Morehouse was one of the best I ever made. And not just because of the great education I received there. My years there provided great inspiration from three different sources: the fact that it was all male and all black; the fact that so many of its graduates had succeeded in a myriad fields; and the fact that Dr. Benjamin E. Mays was its president. Dr. Mays was a demanding educator and an inspiring leader who had high expectations of his students. His charge to us was challenging: "There is an air of expectancy at Morehouse College. It is expected that the student who enters here will do well. It is also expected that once a man bears the insignia of a Morehouse graduate, he will do exceptionally well. We expect nothing less."

Having graduated from Morehouse in 1967, I was a beneficiary of the civil rights movement. I received twenty-five job offers, and they came from some of America's most respected and successful corporations.

But now, I realized, I had to make good on my potential.

3

Gloria

*Who can find a virtuous woman? For her worth is far
above rubies.*

—Proverbs 31:10

Gloria Etchison was beautiful. Let's face it; I was first at-
tracted by her looks. And then I figured out she was also
smart.

I could say that we met through a mutual friend at a party.
But the true story of how we met—the story she *doesn't* like
for me to tell, because of where that happened—is that we first
laid eyes on each other on a street corner.

My entrepreneurial dad was still working 24/7 at his full-
time job as a chauffeur when he opened a grocery store in
our neighborhood, on a corner where two streets intersected.
When I was a freshman in college, I worked there to earn
money for my tuition.

A friend of mine, a young lady named Ruth that I had gone

to high school with, lived close to the store. One day when there were no customers in the store and I went outside, Ruth was walking up the street with another young lady. I thought: This woman is *gorgeous*! Who *is* she? They finally got up to where I was and Ruth introduced us. It turned out that she was the same young lady Ruth had been wanting me to go on a blind date with. I had refused because I'd never had any luck with that kind of date.

That night, Ruth was giving a party. I went and so did Ruth's friend, but she hardly talked to me. She was about to start her freshman year of college and was more interested in talking to some people who were already going there than in talking to some guy she had just met on a street corner.

She didn't really push me off, but she didn't think I was all that cool either. After all, she didn't know at that time about my ambition or about what I had been involved in during my high school years. It was almost a year before we went out on our first date.

I actually tried to take her out the week after the party, but her mom was sick. I respected the fact that she didn't want to go out because she didn't want to leave her mom. This went on for a while and the next thing I knew, school was starting. She was a freshman at Morris Brown College, and I was going to be a sophomore at Morehouse College.

Then, about a year later, we ran into each other on her campus—students from the different campuses would go to others just for social reasons—and we reconnected. I asked her out and this time she said, "Okay." On our first date, we went to the movies. I don't remember which one, but I do remember *the date*. It was magic from that moment on and so I didn't go out with anyone else. Neither did Gloria. And we dated and dated and *dated*.

Then we made the biggest personal decisions of our lives: I asked Gloria to marry me and she said "yes." I was a senior at Morehouse when we formally got engaged and Gloria was a junior at Morris Brown. After her graduation a year later, we were married. It was June 23, 1968.

Our daughter, Melanie, was born in 1971 and Vincent followed six years later. Later on, when we relocated to Omaha because of my work, they didn't have problems adjusting. They got used to being in the predominantly white school and living in the predominantly white environment, because they really hadn't known anything else.

But Gloria and I used to talk with Melanie and Vincent about what it was like in the segregated South when we were growing up. They couldn't really identify with it. They had more of an historical awareness.

We always insisted on having quality family time at home. We had a rule about turning off the TV and the radio when we had dinner—no boob tube, no boom box—because that's when we talked. That's the way we did it in our family, even when they didn't have anything to say: If it was quiet long enough, they'd start talking.

One day when Vincent was about six or seven—I don't remember exactly how old he was—he asked, "Dad, did they have TV when *you* were growing up?"

I thought: This kid is really out of touch. I said, "Yes, Vincent, they had TV when I was growing up." Then I gave him its history and evolution. I told him that our first TV was very small; that we had only one set and it was black and white, not color; and that the *Ed Sullivan Show*, broadcast every Sunday evening, was the one that everybody watched then.

Just as Sundays were family time when Gloria and I were growing up, they remain so to this day. In fact, in 2011, because I had to leave Atlanta on Sunday, June 12, in order to prepare for the New Hampshire debate the next day, Gloria decided to cook me Sunday dinner on Saturday. The kids came over with the grandkids and Gloria prepared a fork-tender roast, collard greens, green beans, candied yams, hand-shucked corn, and homemade cornbread. That's the meal I want on my deathbed—that is, if I can still eat.

Now, as I continue to travel the country seeking my party's presidential nomination, Gloria continues to be a steady source of devotion and inspiration, never more so than now.

Some people have certain expectations concerning the traditional politician's wife, though, and I'm often asked: "Where is your wife? Why isn't she campaigning with you?"

"She is at home," I answer.

And Gloria will tell them that *she's* not running but she supports me 100 percent. That's all I need.

What it all comes down to is that while Gloria and I are both CEOs of ourselves, we are also vice chairman and vice chairwoman, respectively, of each other's boards of directors. We have shared mutual advice and support on key decisions and destination points for more than forty-three years now and the love we share is *priceless*.

4

Mathematics to Pepperoni

Seek ye the LORD, while he may be found, call ye upon him while he is near.

—Isaiah 55:6

When I married Gloria, I was already working as a mathematician with the Department of the Navy, in Dahlgren, Virginia. My mom wasn't happy when I told her that I had accepted that job. She kept saying, "Why do you have to go all the way up there for a good job. Aren't there good jobs in Atlanta?"

"You don't pick a job for that reason," I explained to her. She and Dad, like many other folks back then, viewed a job as your career. To them, you worked for thirty-five years; got a gold watch; and you retired. I've had five careers, but Mom didn't understand the multiple-career concept.

I didn't know then how many jobs I was going to have, but I

knew I wasn't going to get a job just to get one and be stuck there if I didn't enjoy it. That wasn't *me*. Mom finally got used to it.

It wasn't long before I realized that my coworker, a white man, was always promoted about a month before I was, despite the fact that I consistently received the same outstanding performance ratings that he did.

One day, I decided to find out why. I asked my boss about it and he said, "It's because you don't have a master's degree." Right then and there, I decided to remove that barrier to my advancement; I would go for a degree in computer science, one of the fastest-growing professions in government and in business during the 1960s and 1970s.

While I applied for admission to several graduate computer science programs, the one I really wanted to attend was Purdue University's. My reasons were twofold: First, I had read that Purdue had one of the top five computer science programs in the country. The second, and more telling reason, given my competitive spirit, was that my boss in the Department of the Navy didn't think I would be accepted there. According to him, even if I did manage to be accepted, I would never be able to finish the program because one had to maintain a B average there—3.0 out of a possible 4.0 for all courses. But I *was* accepted, and with the transfer of two classes and credits from another university, I completed my graduate studies in one intense, demanding year, earning a degree in computer science.

Did I consider for one moment that my boss was right about me? Could he have stopped me in my tracks? No, absolutely not! Remembering that I was CEO of Self, I was able to reject his opinion and advice because I remembered what Mr. Johnson, my high school math teacher, had told me about having to work *a little harder, and a little longer.*

That is exactly what I did, compiling a 3.4 grade point average and earning my master's degree. My determination to attend Purdue helped me to get my job at Coca-Cola, because Bob Copper, a native Hoosier, knew firsthand of the university's outstanding reputation.

I would never have known the real story about my not having been promoted had I not invoked my right as CEO of Self to ask: *Why* am I being passed over for advancement? By dealing with that instance of discrimination, as well as with so many other negative things in my life, I chose as CEO of Self to remove the barriers rather than to allow the barriers to remove me.

I would have to deal with another form of discrimination during my time at Dahlgren: even after major civil rights legislation had been passed, I couldn't get a haircut in the barber shop of my choosing. Thinking that I wouldn't have a problem in Fredericksburg because I knew of a place there that employed black barbers, I drove over there and went in.

There were people in all the chairs—white people—so I sat down to await my turn. Other patrons, all of them white, came, had their haircuts, and left, but half an hour later, I was still awaiting *my* turn. Every other customer had been told "next"—except for *me.* I asked one of the barbers why I had not been called, and he told me that they were not allowed to cut black people's hair there.

When I left that barbershop, I bought a set of clippers and

cut my own hair. I continue to cut my own hair to this day, exercising my right as CEO of Self to do so.

I was happy at my job as a Navy mathematician. I was twenty-seven years old and managing a group of professionals and I even achieved my ambition of earning $20,000 a year. My five-and-a-half years with the department were, by most standards, a genuine success, so I reasoned that moving up from my current status as a GS-13 to a GS-14 would be more of a function of time than opportunity.

My long-term goal was to become a corporate executive, so much so that one day, I said aloud, "I want to be vice president of something, for somebody, somewhere, someday."

And, of course, the logical place to begin to realize my goal was at Coca-Cola, Dad's place of employment. I was interviewed there by Bob Copper, the head of a corporate analysis group in Atlanta, but he told me that no jobs were available.

Two weeks later, however, he called and invited me to meet with his boss and some other people. Bob said that as a result of my exceeding his expectations in our first meeting, he was trying to convince his boss to create a position for me. He succeeded, and I came aboard.

Some of my friends thought that leaving government employment was a risky move. They pointed out that I was giving up a comfortable and secure position. While I welcomed their advice, only I, as CEO of Self, could decide what to do. As it turned out, my decision to change direction turned out to be the right one. Although I had the title of manager of management science, my position at Coca-Cola was really being a project manager, which was a great starting point for my entrance into the corporate world, as I was involved in some very interesting projects and I learned the basic concepts and language of business.

After four years at Coca-Cola, however, I was becoming stuck in neutral. What I really wanted to do was to become a vice president. But I was not on the right track to achieve *that* goal. I realized that to have any chance of becoming a vice president, I would have to stay there for a long time, paying my dues by working in the trenches and earning my stripes by consistently delivering bottom-line positive profit and loss results.

And there was another obstacle to my advancement at Coca-Cola: As I suspected, my being known as the "chauffeur's son" would always limit my future opportunities there.

As luck would have it, Bob Copper, who had joined the Pillsbury Company in Minneapolis three years after my arrival at Coca-Cola, invited me to come on board there. When I asked why he had chosen me over many other competent people in his Coca-Cola group, he said that I was more of a risk-taker than they were, and that there was some risk in what he was trying to accomplish at Pillsbury.

"What will happen to us if we don't succeed?" I asked.

"The two of us will be looking for new jobs," he replied.

I have always been more motivated by the possibility of success than by the fear of failure, so what Bob said didn't scare me off and I accepted his offer. My dad was fine with that. While he knew that Coca-Cola had given me a good start in the private sector, he realized that the company probably wasn't going to allow me to move up in the organization the way I wanted to—that as long as I remained there, I was always going to be viewed in that predominantly white corporate culture as *his son*, not as the mathematician and computer scientist I actually was.

I was thirty-two years old when I came on board at Pillsbury, and I set my next "decade goal" to reach vice presidential status by the time I turned forty. I realized that by setting and achieving a series of decade goals, those "biological clock blues" on reaching forty or fifty would not be such a big deal.

I reported to Bob Copper at first, and when Bob became vice president for strategic planning, I reported to Dr. John Haaland, Pillsbury's corporate vice president of systems. John Haaland and Bob Copper were true CEOs of Self.

I advanced quickly. In a matter of years, I moved from manager to director; from director to group director; and from group director to senior director of Management Information Systems for the Consumer Products Division.

My biggest leadership challenge in that post came when Pillsbury acquired the Green Giant Company. I was responsible for integrating its MIS department into our Consumer Products Division's MIS department. There were obvious redundancies in systems and positions that had to be eliminated without disrupting services. My task was particularly challenging: If we did not execute the integration smoothly, we could shut down the day-to-day operations of the largest and most profitable division of the company.

Fortunately, that integration went as smoothly as silk. One year later, when Dr. Haaland called me to let me know that he was leaving the company to pursue *his* dream, he told me that

I had been selected to replace him as corporate vice president of systems.

I now had two major challenges. The first one involved a three-part effort: getting approval from the company's board of directors to build a new, multi-million-dollar, state-of-the-art data processing facility; getting the new mainframe computer installed; and then making sure that all the systems were running smoothly.

My second, more complex challenge concerned responsibility for the completion of Pillsbury's World Headquarters, then being built by a major real estate developer in downtown Minneapolis, a twin-towered, forty-floor office complex where Pillsbury would be the lead tenant, occupying most of the space.

At that time, Pillsbury's headquarters staff was spread out over nine locations throughout the greater Minneapolis area. In addition to requirements for the executive officers and for various corporate functions, space was also needed for the agricultural, consumer products, international, and restaurant divisions, as well as for several smaller business units.

It wasn't long before I realized what a decision-making, coordination, and communications nightmare my assignment was turning out to be! This project was over budget, behind schedule, and headed for a "crash" with our future landlord. Language ambiguities in the lease contract caused conflicts over who would be responsible for paying for changes to the project—and we're not talking peanuts, but millions of dollars in *real* money.

I asked the previous executive in charge, who was retiring,

to call a meeting so that I could meet everyone responsible for various pieces of the project. Walking into a conference room where more than twenty people were sitting around a large table, I wondered: Who *are* all these people?

I soon found out. There sat a chief accountant, a chief architect, a chief attorney, a chief construction consultant, a chief contractor, a chief engineer, a chief moving manager, a chief planner, as well as all of their *cochiefs*! Said "chiefs" looked at me as if to say: So how are you, a young whipper-snapper, going to straighten out this mess?

Frankly, I had no idea! This was supposed to be just a get-acquainted session, so I hadn't had the opportunity to speak with each chief separately in order to identify the right problems to deal with. The only thing that Dr. Haaland and I knew at that moment was that the World Headquarters Project was an all-consuming *mess*!

I began my job of straightening things out by discussing with Bill Spoor and Win Wallin, Pillsbury's president and CEO and COO, respectively, not only what they wanted to see, but what they *did not* want to see in the new World Headquarters.

Given their input, I was not afraid to take charge, make decisions, and focus on the critical things I needed to do in order to get the project moving. Again, seeing myself as CEO of Self, I was determined not to fall into a comfort zone of letting other people, no matter how competent and well-meaning, make the decisions for me.

As a result—treating the individual chiefs as a kind of board of directors—the World Headquarters Project was completed ahead of schedule and under budget. Five years later, Bill Spoor presented me with the Pillsbury Company's Symbol of Excellence in Leadership Award.

After the headquarters project turned out successfully, I was once again bored. Life was good—Gloria and I were healthy; we now had a daughter and a son; we lived in a nice home; we had even started taking vacations, which we had never done much earlier in my career. I was even singing in the church choir and recording with a Minneapolis gospel singing group. But my motivation had collapsed.

I was sitting in my new office on the thirty-first floor of the World Headquarters one day when I looked out the window and saw that the inflatable dome of the new Minneapolis stadium had collapsed. I realized, as I sat there, staring out the window, that what had kept me happy and motivated was the excitement, challenge, and risk of the past few years.

I also thought about Dad, who had always been one of my heroes and was then dealing with the complications of diabetes. I thought about how much he had been able to accomplish in his life with a lot less than I had started with, and what a difference he had made to so many people, especially to *me*.

I was thirty-six years old and although I had been blessed to achieve so much, so fast, I knew at that moment that I had to reach for *more*. So I began to imagine how exciting it would be if I were actually the decision-maker running a business!

So as CEO of Self, after several successful years as vice president of Pillsbury's corporate systems and services, I knew that I had to dream higher: I had to dream of being *president* of something, for somebody, somewhere. And I decided to put that dream into action.

Achieving that dream meant that I had to change careers. Although I had run a very important staff function for Pillsbury, I did not have experience with profit and loss, or P&L responsibility for a business unit.

I consulted Win Wallin and he advised me that my path to becoming president of a business unit lay within one of Pillsbury's rapidly growing restaurant companies, and he suggested that I explore the possibility of going to work for Burger King.

It was easy for Win to say that, but my going to Burger King would mean the loss of my hard-earned, and much coveted, vice presidential title; a significant initial drop in salary; loss of stock options; the need to learn a new business from the ground up; and, if I succeeded, a potentially disruptive relocation to another part of the country.

Fortunately, Gloria, always my greatest supporter, understood my need to undertake this new challenge and she was with me every step of the way.

But Mom thought I had lost my mind: "You're a vice president and now you're going to make *hamburgers*?" she demanded.

"I'm not going to make hamburgers forever," I explained. "I just have to learn so I can move up the corporate ladder."

As I had predicted, I had to work my way up the corporate ladder again. I've always been inspired by a new challenge; I was never happy being in cruise control. One of the things that always challenged me the most was doing something that people say you *shouldn't* do.

After meeting with Burger King's president and some key executives, I was offered the opportunity of entering the company's "fast track" program. If I completed the eighteen-month program successfully, I could then be made vice president and regional general manager—a crucial step in my aim for a company presidency, as I would be given full P&L responsibility for my assigned region.

Several weeks later, I received a description of the fast track program in writing, along with an offer to join the Burger King Corporation. I assured Gloria that we would not starve if things did not work out there because I was not too proud to work any job I had to in order to take care of her and our children.

But if this move to Burger King *did* work out, who knew where it could lead? Once again, the possibility of success was motivating me more than the fear of failure.

In deciding whether to leave my comfortable corporate VP job at Pillsbury to start over at Burger King, I asked myself one question, the *right* question: Will this put me in a better position to become president of a business? I did not ask myself the wrong questions: How hard will my new job be? What will my friends think if they see me making hamburgers in a quick-service restaurant? What will I do if this new position does not work out as planned? As a CEO of Self, I knew that those questions were not the right ones to be asking. I focused on my dream and I accepted the offer to join the company's fast track program, with no guarantees.

The people I worked with at Pillsbury gave me a farewell reception in a large activities room near my office. During the party, my secretary came over to me and said there was an urgent telephone call for me. My brother, Thurman, was on the line. "Dad just passed away," he said.

While we had been expecting that sad news, the finality of it was very real. I just sat there for a few minutes and prayed. Then I collected myself and returned to the reception. I knew that was what Dad would have wanted me to do.

I've always had a philosophy whenever I've changed jobs or careers: Never look back, no matter how hard it gets. So on the day I left Pillsbury for the last time, I never looked back. I knew that there had been a message for me in Dad's having passed during my farewell party: I had to succeed. I was motivated to do so.

· · · · · · · · ·

I began my career at Burger King by reporting to the Bloomington training restaurant in the Minneapolis region, where I was issued a crew uniform, a set of operations manuals, a training manual, and my schedule for the week.

I started my fast track training at the back of the place, where I was responsible for putting buns and patties through the broiler. Assignment to one's next position would be based on developing some proficiency, and before the end of that first day, I was assigned to the front of the broiler, to learn the steamer position, and I was off and running.

I would eventually progress through all the positions in the restaurant. After spending a few weeks in the "back of the house," learning the broiler, steamer, burger board, whopper board, specialty sandwich board, and fry station, I moved to the "front of the house," working the positions of cashier, expediter, drive-through order taker, runner-bagger, and drink station operator.

Not long afterward, I spent a week of classroom operations instruction at the regional training center for assistant managers. Then, following more restaurant practice and classroom training, I went to Miami for ten days of study at Burger King University, a structured training center at the company's headquarters.

Burger King University was very well organized and very well run. There were sixty to seventy people in a class, from all over the country. Burger King had ten regions, and each one would send some of their assistant managers.

I was the only former corporate vice president in the class; all the rest of them were either college graduates entering the restaurant industry or people who had started out working in a restaurant and worked their way up to an assistant manager's position. Most of them just wondered: Why is *he* here?

The training program was very structured and very good, and it reinforced some of the basic information we were supposed to have known before we got there. But it was also designed to drive us a little further, to give us more of a restaurant manager's training, because the main reason we were going was that we were all assistant managers aspiring to be managers or managers aspiring to be district managers.

We went to class literally all day, for five straight days, in a very intensive training environment. We'd have lectures, homework assignments, in-class exercises, exams, and tests, as well as guest speakers. I tried to befriend those guys. And I did, especially when we got into that management stuff, because I'd already been a vice president of a corporation and already knew some of those management principles. So I actually mentored them a bit—at least the ones who wanted to listen.

I enjoyed it because my focus was always on where I was trying to get to, never on where I had *been*: I wanted to be a vice president and regional general manager of Burger King and I needed to go to Burger King University. I never worried that I would have to make hamburgers and fries. I didn't care about that, as long as they thought that was necessary for me to get to where I wanted to go. And I never regretted switching companies.

Once I had successfully completed my in-restaurant and classroom training, I was assigned to the Hopkins, Minnesota, unit as fourth assistant manager. At the age of thirty-six, I was that "old dude"—the subject of speculation by the managers and assistants as to why I was being fast tracked to become a regional vice president.

My first test of fire came when a usually dependable young Asian man working the steamer position during the busy lunch period accidentally tangled his foot in the flexible gas hose connected to the broiler.

No one noticed at first that the gas to the broiler had been cut off. Then Mary Pat, who was working the burger board, called me in from the front of the restaurant to report that the patties were coming out undercooked. When I went back there to adjust the broiler, I discovered that the dozens of patties coming out of the broiler had not been cooked at all.

I realized that it would take at least fifteen minutes to get the broiler back up to cooking temperature. The lines at the counter were backed up to the front door; the cars in the drive-through lane were wrapped all the way around the restaurant and into the street. We had no burgers at Burger King!

A situation like that had never arisen in the classroom training. I decided on the spot that two things would be required of me: leadership and a common sense approach to dealing with the problem. So, after asking Mary Pat to restart the broiler, I told the person handling the specialty sandwiches station to make as many chicken and fish sandwiches as fast as the operations manual would allow. Then I told the beverages person to start pouring out soft drinks in all sizes and all flavors as fast as the machine would go. And then I said to the fry station person: "Keep dropping fries until I tell you to stop."

After issuing these orders, I went to the front of the restaurant and informed the customers that it would be fifteen minutes before we would again be serving burgers and Whoppers. Then I went outside, going from car to car to explain the situation. By the time the broiler was up and running, we had sold out of the chicken and fish sandwiches.

I had made it through my first crisis.

When I was appointed as manager of my first Burger King restaurant and asked the regional manager to explain his expectations, he said: "Just increase the sales and the profits." At that time, the end-of-year sales projection for that restaurant was $800,000. When I asked my boss if I could change any of the menu prices, he said, "No." When I asked if I could spend some discretionary marketing dollars, he responded, "No." And when I requested permission to eliminate the Parmesan sandwich—we sold only two a month—he once again said "No."

So as I took charge of the restaurant, I considered the one thing he could not put into a "you cannot do that" category: changing the attitude of all of my employees. I noticed that many of my cashiers were not smiling. At Burger King University we had been advised to tell the cashiers to smile because then the customers would smile and come back. So I established the BEAMER program, which taught our employees, mostly teenagers, how to make our patrons smile.

Within three months of the program's initiation, the sales trend was moving steadily higher, and the district manager raised his sales projection to upward of one million dollars—and I still had that Parmesan sandwich on the menu!

The BEAMER program had a simple but effective premise—look people in the eye and smile, and they will smile back, and it was a huge success. One day, at the end of a lunch shift, a lady who was sitting at a table where she could observe the entire front counter area asked me, "Are you the manager?"

I assumed she had a complaint, because you usually don't expect customers to stop you to say something is good. But she asked, "How do you get so many happy people at the front counter?" I smiled and thought to myself, *"Yes, it's working!"*

· · · · · · · · ·

I did very well at the fast track program, but my transition from vice president at Pillsbury to Burger King regional manager was not as smooth. Not only did I have to deal with resentment and sabotage, but also with a conspiracy to get me fired!

The resentment stemmed from the fact that as a former vice president with the parent company, Pillsbury, it was thought that I would deny a Burger King veteran one of the much-sought-after regional manager positions.

The sabotage occurred in the Minneapolis region when I'd been the manager of a particular restaurant for only a month or so. One night I was working the evening shift, which meant that I had to close down the restaurant at 11:00 P.M. That involved taking the daily inventory, cleaning and sanitizing the equipment, and cleaning the restaurant in preparation for the next day. In addition, as the closing manager, I had to count out and balance the cash receipts with the recorded register receipts and deposit the money in the bank, keeping enough cash on hand to start business the next day.

That night my cash count came up fifty dollars short of my register receipts. I stayed up all night counting and recounting, trying to discover what was wrong. Had I done something wrong? Or were the record tapes incorrect? It was driving me nuts!

Finally, when the opening manager for the next day arrived I gave up and listed the shortage on my daily report. And when I closed the following night, the cash was fifty dollars *over*, which I also included in my report.

It was only during my last week as manager of that restaurant that I learned what had happened: I had been set up in a sting designed to shake me up and to see whether I would operate strictly according to procedure. The assistant manager had removed and then replaced the fifty dollars.

After confessing and apologizing to me for what he had done, the assistant manager explained that it was common knowledge around Burger King that the regional manager wanted me to fail. I accepted the assistant manager's apology. He had come to respect me and to admire my sincerity when dealing with people. We remain friends to this day.

Within three months of my becoming a first-time restaurant manager, sales increased by 20 percent. Then, after completing nine months of the usual eighteen-month fast track program, I was pulled out and made regional vice president (RVP) of the Philadelphia Region. After a year and a half as RVP, and despite my region exceeding its performance goals, a conspiracy to get me fired was hatched in the company's corporate headquarters. The conspiracy failed.

The reason I did so well in running Burger King's Philadelphia region is that I treated people like *people* and the culture at Burger King was intimidation, fear, and screaming, tactics to which I do not subscribe. I believe in telling people when they're doing something right.

After my reassignment to Philadelphia, my new boss, Bill DeLeat, a true CEO of Self, paid my region a visit and spent three days intensively examining its operations. He then told me it was one of the best, if not *the* best-performing region in the country.

In retrospect, the unexpected obstacles I encountered at Burger King may have been a blessing in disguise. Had I anticipated them up front, I might have lost sight of my dream. Instead, I focused on the problems as they came to light. That's what CEOs do all the time: solve problems so that they can move on—and stay *focused*.

In 1986, four years after having taken over Burger King's Philadelphia Region, I was attending an RVP meeting in San Francisco when I had a telephone call from Jeff Campbell, the executive in charge of Pillsbury's restaurant companies—in other words, the boss of my boss's boss.

Jeff asked me to meet him in Miami. He wanted to discuss the possibility of my taking over Godfather's Pizza, Inc., a company that Pillsbury had recently acquired.

5

The Godfather's Years:
From CEO to Entrepreneur

But without faith it is impossible to please Him:
for he that cometh to God must believe that He is;
and that He is a rewarder of them that diligently seek Him.
—Hebrews 11:6

That fateful call from Jeff Campbell, made from the company's headquarters in Miami, Florida, would lead to my achieving my wildest dream: becoming president of *something.*

What Jeff Campbell *didn't* say when he called me from Miami was that Godfather's was on the verge of bankruptcy. It had been acquired by Pillsbury in 1985 as part of its agreement to purchase Diversifoods, Inc. To acquire the nearly three hundred Burger King units owned and operated at that time by Diversifoods, Pillsbury had to include Godfather's in that deal.

I had never been to Omaha before, or to Nebraska, for that matter. On April 1, my first day on my new job, the initial item on my agenda was to meet with Jan, my new executive assistant, and with Ron Gartlan, Godfather's executive vice president of corporate support.

The next thing on my schedule that day was to attend an orientation meeting. While waiting for it to get underway, I wandered into the employees' lunch area. A young lady was sitting there and we began to chat.

"Are you new here?" she asked.

"Yes," I said. "I'm Herman Cain and this is my first day."

"I'm Lori Williams and I work in accounts receivable," she informed me. "What will *you* be doing here?"

"I'm the new president of the company," I replied.

"I've heard every line in the book, but this is a *new* one," she said. "You're the president of the company? Get out of here. Who are you trying to kid?"

We both laughed and then she said she had to get back to work. When Pillsbury announced that I was the new president, they did not include a picture of me.

Later that afternoon, Ron Gartlan called an employees' meeting to introduce me to everyone working in the corporate office. As I began to speak, I noticed that somebody sitting in the back of the room was hiding behind the person sitting in front of her, trying not to be seen. I leaned to one side to get a better look. There sat Lori Williams, so I said, "Hi, Lori."

Everybody was surprised at my greeting her by name. After all, it was the first staff meeting of my first day at work, so how could I already know her? And when I described how we had just met in the lunchroom, everybody, except for Lori, thought the story was hilarious. She eventually came round and it was a good ice breaker. I guess that Lori, along with everybody else, realized that her new boss had a sense of humor.

I then spoke about my background, career, and business philosophy, stressing that I was not coming to Godfather's with answers to all the company's problems. Rather, my job would be to help formulate and then implement a plan of action. And I made it clear that I would not have come to Godfather's unless I had been convinced that the company could once again be successful.

Introductions accomplished, it was time for me to get to work. I knew as I did so that in order to reboot Godfather's, I would have to muster all my analytical skills; apply my philosophy of "exceeding the expectation of the job"; and, according to my overriding principle, "Focus, focus, focus."

My efforts, against all odds, to bring the company back to profitability bore fruit within eighteen months. But first I had to readjust my sights. It's one thing to want to be the president of a large enterprise, but it's another thing to get to be one. And it's quite another thing to actually arrive at your new office, sit at your desk, and *be* that president. In my particular case, taking over Godfather's was especially challenging, given the company's negative growth and declining sales.

I followed that first staff meeting with a one-on-one with my predecessor. I was taken aback when he neglected to talk about "QSC"—quality, service, and cleanliness—based on my experience at Burger King, the three requirements that are the heart of the restaurant business.

If an operation is not consistent in QSC, the question is not *if* you will go out of business, but *when*. My predecessor's failure to speak of QSC during our discussion was my first indication that the "right questions" had never been asked. And, likely, that the right problems had not been identified.

That evening, after a long and exciting day, I had dinner with Ron Gartlan. Having been with the company since 1982, he had witnessed just about everything that had happened at Godfather's since then, including the parade of four presidents who had only briefly "touched down" within three years.

Our conversation was direct and open. In response to one of my questions, Ron said, "I don't know if you are going to keep me around, but I'm going to tell you the truth anyway." I knew instinctively that he was extremely trustworthy—a person I would keep on my team. And my instinct was right: Ron proved to be thoughtful, analytical, responsive, and, most important, brutally honest.

The rest of my first week at Godfather's was taken up with one-on-one meetings with the company's top twenty executives in as many hours; visits to several of our Omaha-area restaurants; and conversations with local franchisees. While some of them were courteous, friendly, and constructive with their feedback about what needed to be done, others were downright rude and hostile.

Those discussions were very informative in helping me to understand why Godfather's business was declining. Now I had a sense of the direction we needed to follow in order to get the company moving in the right direction again.

Then I asked each one of the executives: "What would you do if you were president of Godfather's Pizza, Inc.?"

While they differed somewhat in their specific answers, they all expressed things like the need for focus, consistency, and leadership. We were on the same page! As a result of listening to the people closest to the situation, I now had a rapidly evolving picture in my head of what needed to be done.

One of the most encouraging conversations I had during that first week was with two franchisees, John Chisholm and Jim Morrisey, who at the time controlled thirty-three units, and they would soon add another thirty-five. Despite Godfather's problems, their operations were among the few successful ones.

We met at their restaurant at Seventy-sixth and Pacific streets. The most important words I heard them say were: "For the good of the system, you might have to require us to do some things we don't want to do." Those words were inspiring! They understood that times had changed; that we had to become a system; and that to do so, Godfather's, as the franchisor, had to take the lead.

I realized pretty quickly that if we were to compete with our three major competitors—Pizza Hut, Domino's, and Little Caesar's, companies with 4,500, 2,800, and 900 units respectively—we would have to determine our strategic focus and then begin the process of getting the whole organization focused.

So during a meeting with sixty district managers and a number of vice presidents, I asked them what came to mind when I mentioned our three competitors. When I said "Pizza

Hut," their responses included the words "red roofs," "our biggest competitor," "all things to all people," and "deep pockets." As for Domino's, their nearly unison response was one word: "delivery." And regarding Little Caesar's, they said, "two for one" and "low price."

I then asked them, "When I say 'Godfather's Pizza,' what comes to mind?" There was silence, so I asked, "Well, what did Godfather's *used* to stand for?" Silence again. Finally, one of the district managers spoke up: "Quality," he said.

It was obvious to me: If my district managers were uncertain about our identity, our customers must also be confused. Now I was sure that what somebody had said during my first one-on-one meetings was accurate: Godfather's had a blurred image.

To turn things around, I suggested that we *refocus* on quality. After all, that's what helped make Godfather's successful in the first place, when a consumer survey had shown that Godfather's overall ratings for good taste and product quality perceptions were high relative to those of our largest competitors.

I said that rather than trying to be the biggest, "We should just be the best." Instead of trying to deliver faster than Domino's, I said, "Lets give our customers the best pizza—when it *gets* there." Instead of trying to be the cheapest, I said, "Let's give our customers the best value for their money."

Now there were nods of approval, even some smiles. I thought: My district managers realize that I know what I'm talking about!

My next move was to challenge all departments to develop plans for reestablishing "quality" as Godfather's special niche.

Then, having established a clear focus on quality, priorities for marketing, product research, new unit development, training, operations, and all respective departmental functions, I knew that consistent quality could be maintained more effectively and productively.

And it wasn't long before the entire Godfather's organization began to resonate with the idea of focus. In fact, by the end of April, my first month on the job, we had pulled together our first tactical action plan to reinvigorate our reputation for quality products. And there were new initiatives, like our pizza-by-the-slice project.

Godfather's now had a new sense of decisiveness and direction. People like to succeed, and they know they can't do that if they don't have direction. As the famous humorist Will Rogers once said, "Even if you are on the right track, you'll get run over if you just sit there."

Ron Gartlan, who I've said is a fellow CEO of Self, had urged me to be visible, since people are inspired when they hear directly from their leader. By both spreading the focus message and challenging people for even more ideas about how we could win again, I learned more about the pizza business in general, and about Godfather's strengths and weaknesses, in particular. And the more I learned, the better my own morale grew.

In order to survive against our much larger competitors, to distinguish our innovative attitude from the old paradigm, and to get our new program off the ground, we developed a *focus* logo. It was a symbol of our new thinking, and we featured it on T-shirts, caps, paperweights, marketing plans, and everywhere else imaginable.

We also developed a "guerilla warfare" atmosphere in order to communicate a sense of urgency to the staff about the necessity of competing, in the words of two marketing gurus, Al Reis and Jack Trout, "to achieve the greatest impact with a small arsenal of competitive weapons."

Winning is the biggest boost there is to morale. And we could win again!

Within sixty days of my coming on board at Godfather's, I suggested that we hold an all-systems meeting to share information about our new focus, projects, and priorities. That meeting was held on May 29, 1986, and the turnout was tremendous.

We discussed many specifics during that daylong gathering. I then closed with an inspirational message, calling upon everybody present to dream again of possibilities beyond their grasp, and challenging them to dream once again of success, prosperity, and personal fulfillment:

When you allow yourself to dream, you look at a mound of clay and see a masterpiece. You look at a glass of water half-empty as a glass half-filled. When you dream again, you are able to recognize that problems are merely opportunities that could unlock the doors to your success. When you dream again, you view today as the first day of the rest of your life. I challenge you to dream of Godfather's as the number-one pizza chain in the world. And if you truly do dream of being a part of that achievement, your creative energies will be unleashed and unstoppable. I challenge you to dream again about what Godfather's can become.

There was more—a concluding challenge to every Godfather's corporate employee, operator, owner, restaurant manager, and crew member, to everyone connected to the Godfather's system: "Let's go. Let's get on with rewriting the currently anticipated future of Godfather's in the annals of the restaurant industry."

But I was not done yet. I said: "There are generally three kinds of people in the world. People who make things happen, people who watch things happen, and people who say, 'What in the heck happened.' People who make things happen—they dream, they commit themselves, they say, 'Let's go!' "

Finally, I cautioned: "In the unforgettable words of my grandfather, a Georgia farmer all his life, who would hitch a team of mules to the wagon on Saturdays for the weekly trip into the local town, 'Them that's going, get on the wagon. Them that ain't, get out of the way.' "

Then, my voice rising to a crescendo, I repeated my grandfather's injunction: "Them that's going, get on the wagon. Them that ain't, get out of the way!"

Most of the people who attended that all-systems meeting "got on the wagon," and our new initiatives began to pay off. But it was several months before our sales increased.

Then I had an idea for a product that could give us a short-term sales boost, so I called my vice president of Research and Development in and asked her: "Can we come up with a product variation that would have great price appeal without sacrificing quality?"

"How *much* appeal do you want it to have," she asked.

"Two large pizzas for twelve dollars—and we still make money," I replied.

A few days later, I was visiting our product development kitchen when I was asked to sample the new product: two large pizzas, with the same quality ingredients, but proportioned differently; my people had come up with both a pepperoni and a four-topping pizza that we could sell at a great price and still achieve a quality product.

We decided to go ahead and roll out the new product—we called it "Big Value"—in as many of our restaurants as possible, and it took off like a rocket! To say it exceeded our expectations is an understatement: Our customers now had a compelling reason to stop in at Godfather's stores, and within a matter of months, many units were hitting new sales records.

While "Big Value" generated great excitement and boosted company morale, we didn't take our focus off our other initiatives. Their success would ensure that we could keep those customers who had rediscovered Godfather's. My first year's results as president of Godfather's exceeded all expectations: We achieved a true turnaround.

Nevertheless, as Ron and I worked to pull together a new strategic plan, we realized that our parent company had reservations about our remaining a subsidiary. Our suspicions about that were confirmed when, following our presentation to top management in which we detailed our great results for the year, no one offered to take us to dinner. Nor was there any in-house celebration in our honor.

So Ron and I went to dinner by ourselves and as we discussed the reactions, comments, questions, and even the body language, we reconfirmed our view that Godfather's days as a Pillsbury subsidiary were numbered.

The story doesn't end there. We hatched a crazy idea: If Pillsbury decided to sell Godfather's Pizza, Inc., we would be its buyers! And while neither of us had ever dreamed of doing so before, I asked Ron rhetorically, "How hard could that be? After all, I've bought a house before."

Four months later, in January 1988, we learned how hard buying a whole company can really be. Jerry Levin, the company's executive vice president of acquisitions and divestitures, called and asked us to meet him the next day in Minneapolis. We did, and, as expected, Jerry informed us officially that Pillsbury had, indeed, decided to sell Godfather's. Although the news was expected, I was still stunned; I felt as if I were being fired.

But sometimes seemingly negative things turn out to be for the best. As I had learned from my parents and grandparents, if one door closes, another door opens, so the best course is to believe in yourself and to look for the next open door. In other words, I once again had to exercise my power as CEO of Self. Pillsbury's decision to jettison Godfather's gave me and Ron Gartlan the opportunity to own the company. For me, that meant going up yet another corporate rung, to CEO.

Two weeks after our meeting in Minneapolis, with Jerry Levin's help, we negotiated Godfather's purchase price. Then we had to find financing. Given Godfather's turbulent financial history of late, that wasn't easy.

Working with a consultant on leveraged buyouts, we made

presentations to nineteen banks and other potential lending institutions. The individual sessions lasted from half a day to three-quarters of a day, with many of our presentations made in our Omaha offices so that potential lenders could visit our local units and sample our products. Then after three months, CitiBank said yes.

Finally, on the morning of September 21, 1988, after nearly nine months trying to obtain our financing, and after signing what seemed to us to be thousands of documents, we closed on our transaction at the Citicorp offices in New York City.

Ron and I, and our very able attorney, Gary Batenhorst, flew to Tampa, where we had scheduled another all-systems meeting. On entering the meeting room, we shook hands. Then I moved to the microphone. After formally greeting everybody, I announced: "At approximately twelve-thirty this afternoon, we closed on a leveraged buyout and we are now the heavily in debt owners of Godfather's Pizza, Inc. Let the real celebration party begin!"

Although Ron and I were very excited at becoming owners, we were now facing challenges beyond simply running a business. We could no longer turn to Pillsbury for cash or capital investment, nor would we have access to our former parent company's reservoir of corporate expertise.

The full impact of being CEO didn't really sink in until we arrived back at Godfather's: I was forty-two years old and I had just made the biggest business decision of my life. I knew that my actions would now affect not only all of Godfather's employees and their families, but the franchisees and their families, as well. As the new owners of Godfather's Pizza, Inc., Ron and I were now responsible for maintaining its vitality and generating the paychecks of more than ten thousand employees, as well as our own. Those realities were sobering.

I was fortunate to have Ron there as my associate. He's one of the most effective and tenacious negotiators I've ever worked with—and his integrity is beyond reproach.

We're very much alike in many ways, having the same values about life and family. But we're also just about as different as two people can be: I'm an extrovert—I'll seize any podium in sight—while Ron is more of an introvert and won't make a speech unless he absolutely has to. But when he does get up on that podium, he does a great job.

Part of my functioning as a pizza company CEO involved knowing about our product. I learned early on about quality ingredients, for instance, what makes a good "all meat" pizza: If the ingredients are not exactly the best quality, all that meat tastes salty. So the way I test a good pizza is to order the "all meat" one. If it tastes too salty, I know that the meat is not top quality. But if you get top-quality ingredients and put them all together, you'll find, like on a Godfather's pizza, it doesn't taste salty. That's one of the little keys to understanding "Pizzaology."

As I went about fulfilling my CEO's responsibilities, I realized more than ever before the meaning of the expression "the buck stops here." Some people didn't grasp that fact, like a former colleague who called me and asked, "So whom do you report to now?"

To be successful, a CEO must answer that question with only one word: "Myself!" That is, if one is a true CEO of Self.

Working together, Ron Gartlan and I were able to put Godfather's Pizza, Inc., back on the success track, with stores throughout the country. It was a great ride, one I'll always remember—and one I absolutely thank God for.

Now, as I travel the country, campaigning for America's highest office, I see parallels between the situation that existed at Godfather's when I came on board and the state of our union today.

The good news is: Being a true CEO of Self to whom God has entrusted yet another opportunity to turn a seemingly impossible situation around, I believe passionately that I will succeed in doing my part to make our great nation whole again.

6

New Challenges
and Achievements

*Have I not commanded thee? Be strong and of good
courage; for the LORD thy God is with thee withersoever
thou goest.*

—Joshua 1:9

M y success at Burger King and Godfather's led to the recognition of my business savvy and financial acumen.
This was demonstrated, starting in 1991, by my appointments
to the corporate boards of major corporations: Nabisco, Super
Valu, Inc., UtiliCorp United, Inc., and Whirlpool; by my selec-
tion in 1994 as chairman of the board and president of the National Restaurant Association; by my appointment in 1995 as
chairman of the Federal Reserve Bank of Kansas City; by my
service during the 1996 presidential campaign as an adviser to
the Dole-Kemp ticket; and by my recruitment in 1998 as CEO

of RetailDNA, a start-up technology company focusing on smart marketing applications for retail businesses.

I also established my own leadership consulting company, T.H.E., Inc. in 1996, which used my skills as a communicator to connect with individuals outside the corporate world. I did this through my radio call-in talk show and by giving speeches. During my tenure as vice president of the National Restaurant Association, I had an attention-getting encounter with Bill Clinton, challenging and stumping the then-president on the issue of health care.

That encounter came about as the result of a telephone inquiry on April 6, 1994, from Loretta Carroll, a news anchor with KMTV in Omaha. She was asking for my reaction to a comment that President Clinton had made the night before during a town meeting in South Carolina. He had said, in essence, that he could not understand the restaurant industry's intense opposition to his health care plan.

The president had insisted that under his scheme, the cost to restaurants would be only about two-and-one-half percent of their cost of doing business. I told Loretta that his observation was ludicrous. I knew that because I had consulted with the staff of the NRA, and they had found Mr. Clinton's calculation to be mathematically incorrect.

Then Loretta told me that in order to maximize diverse participation at the president's town meeting, scheduled to take place the next evening in Kansas City, it had been decided that while the program would originate in Kansas City, there would also be live pickups from Omaha, Topeka, and Tulsa, and she asked whether I would like to participate from Omaha.

When I told Loretta that I would be happy to do so, she asked whether, if given the chance, I would be prepared to ask the president a question. When I responded that I would, Loretta, who knew how passionate I can be when I believe in an issue, advised me to "be respectful."

"Of course I will," I promised.

The next night, I joined approximately one hundred people gathered at KMTV's West Omaha studio. When the telecast began, the president took an initial round of questions from each city. While I did not participate in that round, it gave me a feel for the program's format, as well as a sense of Mr. Clinton's style in such a setting.

The early questions seemed platitudinous, emotional, and not very factual. I was determined that if given the opportunity to pose a question, I would address something concrete concerning the president's plan: I was not going to waste his time, or, for that matter, mine, by tossing him a softball.

When Omaha's turn came around once again, Loretta said, "Mr. President, the CEO of Godfather's Pizza is here and he has some concern about the cost of health care reform for service industries, specifically restaurants."

It was one of the few times in my life that I felt somewhat nervous. Not because I was going to ask Bill Clinton a tough question and not because I was on a television broadcast. I had been on TV many times in the past. My nervousness stemmed from my respect for the office of the president of the United States. Just before I stood up, and not knowing exactly what I was going to say, I mouthed the words of my favorite prayer, "Not my will, O Lord, but thy will be done."

In my opening remarks, I said, "At your state of the union

speech, you indicated that nine out of ten Americans currently have health care insurance, primarily through their employers. And tonight you indicated that of those people who do not have insurance, eight of ten of them work for someone. And your plan would force employers to pay this insurance for those people that they currently do not cover. I would contend that employers who do not cover employees do not, for one simple reason, and it relates to cost."

I then said that I had calculated what his program would cost Godfather's Pizza. I said that I had also spoken with hundreds of other business people about his program's impact on their operations. "The cost of your program is simply a cost that will cause us to eliminate jobs," I explained. "In going through my own calculations, the number of jobs that we would have to eliminate to try to absorb this cost is a lot greater than I ever anticipated. Your averages about the impact on smaller business—those are well intended—but all of the averages represent a wide spectrum in terms of the businesses impacted."

Getting to the gist of the matter, I said, "On behalf of all those business owners who are in a similar situation to mine, my question is, quite simply, if I am forced to do this, what will I tell those people whose jobs I will have to eliminate?"

Our colloquy continued for four minutes, focusing primarily on what, I informed the president, was his faulty math, and ended with Mr. Clinton's asking me to detail my findings regarding cost in a letter to him. I did so but never received a response from *him*, just one from the head of the Small Business Administration.

My question and my words, "Mr. President, with all due respect, your calculations are incorrect," provoked a tremendous nationwide wave of interest and observation—so much so that when I arrived at my office the next morning, the telephones were ringing off the hook and my staff was hard-pressed to load enough paper into the fax machine to collect all the letters and notes people were sending. Ninety-eight percent of the people who called or sent faxes were supportive of my position and my comments to the president.

While the day was hectic and I just couldn't get off the telephone, there were some amusing moments. One lady kept Jan, my executive assistant, on the phone for twenty minutes, telling her how much she opposed my position on health care and how upset she was that I had disagreed with the president. She was so incensed, in fact, that she told Jan, "I'm never going to go to Domino's Pizza again!" to which Jan responded, "That's a very good idea."

Over the next several months, hundreds of people let me know—either in person or by letter—that my town hall meeting "chat" with President Clinton had inspired them to write or to telephone their congressperson and to believe that because of my initiative, something could be done to stop a government plan that millions of people simply did not believe in.

While I was not the first person who tried to point out to the president and members of his administration how his proposed plan would affect jobs and the economy, my "four minutes of notoriety" would serve as a lightning rod, and would become, in the words of Newt Gingrich, one of my worthy opponents for the Republican Party's presidential nomination in 2012, "the turning point of the debate."

Bill Clinton's—and Hillary's—health care plan failed, only

to be revived in somewhat different form in Massachusetts by Mitt Romney and in the White House by Barack Obama. Neither Hillary Clinton nor Barack Obama had an ounce of common sense when they put their health plans together. The big difference is that the Clinton care bureaucracy was not nearly as bad as Obama's is. Neither one of them asked the people closest to the problem how do we make sure that the issue of health care insurance for everybody becomes simpler while bringing down the cost.

It seems that when it comes to health care legislation, "seasoned" politicians apparently cannot discern the will of the American people.

My own assessment of what people took away from that town meeting was, first, the impression of a calm and confident businessman who *knew what he was talking about* without sounding arrogant or disrespectful—that I was neither the stereotypical ruthless big business executive nor the know-it-all elected official from Washington who, regardless of his perceived political savvy and experience, people had come to distrust.

My encounter with Mr. Clinton demonstrated yet again to me that leadership is not an endowed consequence of positionship, just as singing ability is not an endowed consequence of having a voice. The "stuff" that people see in a leader is not always quantifiable or immediately recognizable. But they know it when they see it—and they know when it is missing.

And now, as I travel the country, I am aware that an increasing number of concerned Americans see this "stuff" in me.

But back then, I wasn't content to rest on those laurels, so I became a political activist, as well as embarking on several new careers, as an author of four books in eight years—*Leadership is Common Sense*, in 1997; *Speak as a Leader*, in 1999; *CEO of SELF*, in 2001; and *They Think you're Stupid*, in 2005 (I'm writing a follow-up to that one)—as a motivational speaker, and as a radio talk-show host.

In Omaha, when I began writing books and giving speeches, I needed a sub chapter S incorporation to separate those activities from my work at Godfather's. The company I formed was called T.H.E., Inc. I came up with that name when, after giving a keynote speech to a large audience, I overheard two ladies talking: "Wow," one of them said, "what a speech by Herman Cain!" And the other lady said, "That wasn't a speech, it was an *experience!*" And that's how I came up with T.H.E., for The Hermanator Experience.

I listened to a customer. What a novel idea!

When I moved to Atlanta, I needed to form a Georgia corporation. But I didn't want to replicate The Hermanator Experience. So, inspired by people coming up to me at conventions and saying, "You have a different way of stating things that's so clear and compelling," I decided to call the new corporation "The New Voice."

The genesis of my involvement with the Federal Reserve stems from my move to Omaha as president of Godfather's Pizza in 1986. I became involved in the community through the Pilgrim Baptist Church, where Gloria and I worshipped. I was soon approached by a man named Joe Edmondson, a quadriplegic confined to a wheelchair. He was thrilled when he found out that I was the "black guy" running Godfather's Pizza, and he pestered my assistant until she gave him an appointment to see me. It wasn't that she resisted doing so; it was simply that there were so many demands on my time.

On the appointed day, Joe and his wife came to my office and he explained that the two of them, operating on a "mom and pop" basis, had put together an organization called the Edmondson Youth Outreach Program. Their idea was to help young, inner-city black kids in North Omaha, where the majority of the city's black families lived, to get off the streets by engaging in various structured activities—for example, a wrestling program.

Joe, who was a father figure to those kids, asked me to join his board. In my experience with not-for-profits, that was code for: Can you help us raise money? I told him that while I wouldn't be able to attend many meetings, I would assist with fundraising. When the news got around that I was getting involved in the community, I received many other, similar invitations.

I ended up joining the board of Creighton University, which included many of Omaha's leading businessmen. I soon received a call from the branch manager of the local Federal Reserve Bank. He was inviting me to lunch, and when we met, he told me about the Federal Reserve, and I eventually joined the board of the Omaha branch of its Kansas City district.

I thought: Wow, the Federal Reserve wants me to serve on one of its boards! That was something I had never really thought about, but it seemed pretty prestigious, so I joined that board, where I served for two years. Then I was asked to serve on the board of the Kansas City District, eventually becoming its chairman.

The meetings of the Kansas City District would usually last for half a day. When I was its chairman, if there was a specific issue that I needed an in-depth briefing on, I would travel from Omaha to Kansas City the afternoon before the meeting to be briefed by the bank's full-time president. Once every few months, I would go to Washington to meet with the Federal Reserve's chairman, Alan Greenspan, and the other governors so they could receive firsthand anecdotal feedback.

Chairman Greenspan was a very amiable, soft-spoken, at times brilliant guy. He would sit patiently and listen to all the reports; hear everybody; and then come to his insightful conclusion about what we needed to do. He was a very effective leader who did not make unilateral decisions.

My service demonstrated to me that we need the Federal Reserve, contrary to what some people, including at least one of my current opponents for the presidential nomination, believe.

I don't believe we need to end the Federal Reserve system—that would be comparable to advocating that we get rid of air traffic controllers because we have some plane crashes. If you do that, you're going to have more crashes. We need to *fix* the Federal Reserve, not end it. That would be a dumb idea!

And to be fair, when I served on the Federal Reserve Board we didn't have a $14 trillion national debt; in those years we had one that totaled $4 to $5 billion, and sometimes less. Initially, its primary mission involved price stability and control of the money supply. Then in the 1970s, the Federal Reserve was charged with managing unemployment. That never should have been done, because you cannot manage unemployment, price stability, and our currency with one arrow, and they had multiple targets but only one arrow.

There are some people who claim that I'm against auditing the Federal Reserve. In the words of my grandfather, "I does not care." That's not one of my lead issues. If somebody wants to audit the Federal Reserve, go ahead and *do* it. I'm not going to make that a top-priority issue for Herman Cain because we have other, more important issues to be concerned about, like jobs and the economy.

Looking back on my time with the Federal Reserve, it gave me the opportunity to be exposed to macroeconomics, to examine and be part of the really big decisions that affect our national economy. I don't apologize for the time I spent on the Federal Reserve. I believe that my colleagues and I collectively performed an honorable, admirable job for the people of this country.

Most of the people who today are vociferous critics of the Federal Reserve system don't know what they are talking about. If you look at its concept purely from a technical, academic standpoint you could conclude that we don't need it since it didn't exist before 1913.

Its critics claim that our money supply and the world's supply will self-regulate. No, they won't. They will not self-regulate, and you will have chaos. Even though I don't agree with everything the Fed has done of late, our currency as it stands today is the world's currency standard. This is why we have to pay down the debt and boost the growth of the economy, so people will stop being nervous about the U.S. dollar.

I wasn't some crazy radical. I knew how to build a responsible business and I always got along with everybody. That's how I got to be head of the Kansas City Federal Reserve. It was another example of Herman just being *Herman*.

As for the National Restaurant Association, or NRA, in 1996, ten years after taking over Godfather's Pizza, I became its full-time, salaried CEO. There, as at Godfather's, I was responsible for leadership in vision, strategy, resources, and execution.

I had been a member of the organization's board since 1988, and had served as its elected volunteer chairman in 1995. It was my accomplishments in that position that led my fellow board members to ask me to take the position of full-time chairman.

However, the challenges of working with a very large board and fifty state associations made communications and consensus building extremely demanding. Whereas the Godfather's board had consisted of the two principal owners—Ron and myself—I would now be chairing a board of seventy-five restaurateurs, all of them elected by the association's general membership. And they encompassed the full range of restaurant categories, including independent and chain operators, as well as operators of full-service, quick-service, and casual dining establishments.

The board members also represented the various priorities of the membership. Full-service operators wanted more National Restaurant Association resources spent on Internal Revenue Service requirements that employers track employees' tips, whereas quick-service chains with their large number of entry-level workers and high turnover rate were more concerned with minimum-wage legislation. Additionally, even though all of the fifty State Restaurant Associations were independent organizations, I needed to maintain a positive working relationship with them if my goals were to be achieved.

I remained CEO of the National Restaurant Association for two-and-a half years, during which time the organization was significantly strengthened, so much so that *Fortune* magazine identified it as the fifteenth most influential association in Washington—the first time the NRA had ever cracked the top one hundred.

When I left the National Restaurant Association in 1999, I was recruited to become the CEO of RetailDNA. The restaurant industry was the first target market for its applications and my mission was to lead in the development of business strategy, organization, and top-level marketing.

In 2000, after accomplishing my goals with RetailDNA, I turned my attention full-time to T.H.E., Inc., my keynote-speaking and leadership consulting company.

As for my career in radio, Martha Zoller, an Atlanta area radio talk show host, started me on it when she asked me to substitute for her. It went so well—this was after my Senate race—that people would call me and say: "You really ought to keep your voice out there."

At the same time, a couple of people who had worked on the campaign suggested likewise, so I asked them to prepare the format for the *Herman Cain Show*. Then I pitched the idea to the general manager of WGKA, a very small Atlanta-area station.

I outlined my concept in a forty-five-minute presentation,

in which I stressed that I planned to deal with major issues. When I finished, the manager said, "Well, you thought about this a bit, didn't you?" Soon after that, I was offered a two-hour program to be aired on Saturdays from 4:00 to 6:00 P.M.

When I started the broadcast, that time slot didn't even have a pulse, but after about a year, the station officials began to notice a blip, like a heartbeat! And they said, "Gee, people are listening."

Then I received a request from WSB to move my show there. As I had no contract with WGKA, I was free to go. There were two considerations that led me to make that decision: First, WSB had an average audience of four hundred thousand listeners while WGKA's was only eighteen thousand.

Second, although the larger station wasn't offering me much money, it was more than the nothing I had been receiving from WGKA. So making the move was a no-brainer.

My new program on WSB was aired on Saturday afternoons from four to six. A year after I started there, I received a diagnosis of cancer and took a year off for treatment. When I came back, the station manager, Pete Spriggs, offered me the noon to 2:00 P.M. slot on Saturdays—the weekend's most-listened-to time-frame.

I would come on the air saying, "If it's high noon, you must be listening to Herman Cain." So I was using the phrase "high noon" years before my Centennial Olympic Park presidential announcement.

As the weeks went by, people began to use that phrase. Dave Baker, the broadcaster who had the very successful show before mine, would close his program by saying, "Stay tuned, here comes that High Noon guy, Herman Cain." After nine months, I was asked to host a five-nights-a-week, three-hours-a-night show, beginning on January 2, 2008. I told them, "That's a *job* and I'm not looking for a *job*." Then they made me an offer I couldn't refuse.

When I asked why I was being given a regular weekday program, I was told my ratings were going up. In addition, I had been one of several people who had subbed for the highly popular personality Neal Boortz, and according to a station survey, I had the highest rating of anyone who had ever substituted for him.

I was given the coveted 7:00 to 10:00 P.M. time slot. In order to do that, WSB moved Michael Savage to the 10:00 P.M. to 1:00 A.M. slot. My ratings were high all the way up to January 2011, when I left the airwaves to pursue my party's presidential nomination.

I can honestly say that if I hadn't been on the radio, I wouldn't have been as familiar with the issues as I am now. Nor would I have thought through common sense solutions for them. There's an old saying: "If you're fat, dumb, and happy, you don't feel like you have to do anything; but if you understand the issues and think you can do something about them, you have an obligation to not just sit there."

I believe that having that program was God's way of forcing me to understand the critical issues confronting our nation. As I carefully listened to what my callers were saying I became very frustrated realizing that the country was on the wrong track. At first, the calls expressed concern, but after the Obama administration had been in office for about a year, the calls of concern became expressions of fear for the future of America. I also felt this fear and decided to do what I could to begin to make things right again.

One night a caller, identifying himself as a young man, said, "Mr. Cain, I'm frustrated."

"*Why* are you frustrated?" I asked.

"Because of the direction of this country and I don't know what to do. Give me some advice."

"Are you a registered voter?" I asked.

"Yes," he answered.

Then I asked him, "Do you vote in all the elections?"

He said "Yes! What else can I do? I'm *frustrated*! I don't know what to do. I can't stop this all by myself."

I'm a firm believer that the Founding Fathers got it right when they penned those great documents, the Declaration of Independence and the Constitution of the United States of America, so I said, "Do you have a copy of the Declaration of Independence?"

He said, "Yes."

I said, "Go get it." Well, he went and got it and came back on the line and I said, "Turn to the part about life, liberty, and the pursuit of happiness—flip, flip, flip, flip—Got it?"

"Got it!"

"Now when you get to the part where it says, 'Life, liberty, and the pursuit of happiness,' here's what you can do to help change things."

"What?"

"Keep reading and you'll find that it says, 'When any form of government becomes destructive to these ends, it is the right of the people to alter or abolish it.' Well, we've got to alter the occupant of the White House and abolish this intrusion of the federal government in our lives; that's what we've got to do. It is not only our right, but our responsibility."

That young man thanked me and I said, "So get involved; get active; do something—everybody can do different things."

7

Beating Stage Four Cancer

Yea, though I walk through the valley of the shadow of
death, I will fear no evil for thou art with me.

—Psalm 23:4

In February 2006, I heard three words that would change my life forever.

I was a member of the board of directors of the Whirlpool Corporation, whose headquarters is located in Benton Harbor, Michigan, and I had been asked to give a speech there as part of the observance of Black History Month. Now, I'm not really fond of Black History Month—why do we only get *a month*? How come we can't we get a whole year? But I know their CEO, and I love their management team, and they said, "Why don't you come up and give a speech to the employees?" So I accepted their invitation.

They always sent one of their company planes to pick me up when I was going to a board meeting, and since this occasion was official corporate business, they sent one to pick me up this time, too.

On the way up to Benton Harbor, I felt a pain in my lower intestine. I thought, "Maybe it's something that I've eaten." When I landed, I immediately went to the restroom. What I didn't know at the time was that I had a tumor in my colon and it had ruptured. I went on and gave the speech, and they flew me back to Atlanta.

I went to my doctor the next day and he said, "You need a colonoscopy, but I can tell you what it sounds like: It sounds like you've got a cancerous tumor in your colon." He was right. I had the colonoscopy and they confirmed it. I found out about that tumor almost purely by accident. If that tumor had not ruptured, I might not have known that I needed to go and get treatment.

The next thing I heard was: "You need to go and get a CAT scan to check out your entire abdomen." So I did that, but they didn't tell me the results. They always want your doctor to give you the results. He did. Then, CAT scan results in hand, I went to see a surgeon, a young lady who had been one for about six years and was recommended by the colonoscopy doctor.

Gloria was with me, and the surgeon talked to us for forty minutes, explaining about my colon cancer and what the re-sectioning procedure was, and on and on and on. Near the end of the conversation, almost as an afterthought, she said, "Now, I don't know what I'm going to do about those tumors in your liver until after I open you up."

"*What* tumors in my liver?" I demanded.

"Oh, you didn't *know*?" she said.

"No," I replied.

Gloria and I were shocked coming out of that surgeon's office. I'll never forget it. That was the first time that I was emotionally shaken. I can deal with stuff if I *know* it. I wasn't shaken when the doctor came in and said, "You've got cancer in your colon." I was ready for that. But when it's thrown at you as a surprise, it's a *shock*.

We were getting into our car—the surgeon's office was only five minutes from where we live—and Gloria asked me, "Are you okay?"

"Yeah," I said.

"Do you need me to drive?" she asked.

"No, I can drive." Then I said, "This is a true test of my faith."

"*Our* faith," Gloria corrected me.

I drove us home and we prayed and then I said, "We'll figure out what we need to do."

I went in to work the next day. I told a young lady who then worked for me, named Ericka, what the results were. She had been doing some research online and she said, "First of all, you need to go to a cancer center, not a hospital that works on cancer." She had already researched Sloan Kettering, in New York, and MD Anderson, in Houston, for me. She said, "Those are the top two in the country. Do you know someone that can help you get into MD Anderson?"

I said, "Yes I do. Boone Pickens, the oil magnate."

I called Boone Pickens, a good friend to this day. He used to be on the board of MD Anderson and was a contributor, and he called the head of the hospital and said, "Herman Cain is not just another person trying to get into MD Anderson; he's also a friend of mine."

After she told me about MD Anderson, my friend Ericka said, "You need a second opinion."

That's when I pushed back. I said, "Why?" I asked. "I had a colonoscopy and they said I have cancer; the surgeon said I have cancer in my liver. Why do I need a second opinion? I'm ready to schedule the surgery."

"You *need* a second opinion!" she insisted. "If you don't get a second opinion, I am going to body-slam you *myself*!"

That was a threat! She was just saying: Get a second opinion to confirm everything that I had already learned because a friend of hers who worked at the National Health Institute said: "Always get a second opinion, no matter what."

It was just the right thing to do—and I didn't want to be body-slammed, because I already had cancer, so I said, "Well, who do you recommend?"

That's when she told me: "Go to see a doctor in Savannah"— Ericka is from Savannah—"he's a colon resection specialist."

"I'm not driving all the way to Savannah, Georgia," I said. "That's way out of the way. Find me a second opinion here in Atlanta."

She insisted, "Go to the one in Savannah!"

"*Why?*"

"His name is Dr. Lord. Be there Monday."

"I'll be there Monday," I said.

So I went to Savannah on Monday to see Dr. Lord. He was very nice. I brought all my files—my CAT scan, colonoscopy results, blood results, chest X-ray results—and he confirmed everything and he said," MD Anderson's the right place to go."

Then he said, "Mr. Cain, go get some lunch. Give me about an hour and a half."

He called in several of his colleagues and they went over all of my results. I went back and talked to him and he didn't charge me a dime—and he supported me in my Senate campaign. He said, "There's something greater that you're supposed to do for this country and this is my contribution."

This all happened in the middle of the week, and we told Melanie and Vincent that weekend. We have family dinners on Sunday, after we go to church, so we told them on that Sunday. We wanted them to be over at the house to explain it to them.

Gloria and I went to Texas and I was admitted to the MD Anderson Center. I was scheduled for an orientation briefing by a particular staff member. However, that lady was busy with another couple, so we were assigned to another briefer. When I meet somebody for the first time, I usually ask that person's name, so I asked this nice lady: "What is your name?"

"Grace," she replied.

Gloria and I looked at each other and smiled. You see, the Lord gives you these road signs—that is, if you know how to recognize them.

Our orientation at an end, they assigned me to an oncologist and a surgeon, who had been chosen at random to treat me. After meeting with the oncologist, we went to the surgeon's office and I asked him, "Since the colon is on one side of the body and the liver is on the other, will you perform two operations?"

"No," he said.

"But don't you have to cut me open on *both* sides," I asked. "If not, how are you going to do this?"

"We do this all the time," the surgeon replied, putting his finger on my chest. "I'm going to make an incision like a 'J.' "

"Like in J-E-S-U-S?" I asked.

"Yes," he said.

I replied, "A 'J' cut!"

I smiled and said, "Thank you, Lord!" That's because when you are in the "Word," you can listen and hear when God is speaking to you.

Just before I began my treatment, I was told by two doctors that I had only a 30 percent chance of surviving. But I had my faith, Gloria right at my side, the support of my family and closest friends, and the determination and belief that I could take the treatment.

Then I had chemotherapy, followed by surgery: the resection of my colon—30 percent of it was removed—and the removal of 70 percent of my liver. More chemotherapy followed. Our ordeal, and Gloria shared every moment of it with me, lasted nine months.

Well, it's been more than six years since then. And guess what? I'm completely cancer-free! *Cured!*

Why was I spared against those odds?

God said, "Not yet!"

Did it have something to do with the Lord wanting me to survive so that I might help set this great nation of ours on its own path of recovery?

I had achieved what I thought was my plan in life.

My journey now is God's plan.

But before my survival came endurance. Gloria, who only a year before my cancer diagnosis had developed a serious heart fibrillation and had to undergo surgery to implant a pacemaker, needed to feel that she had some control over the ordeal we were now facing together. So she began to compile what we called my "cancer timeline."

In doing so, she also brought a measure of comfort to cancer sufferers and their loved ones. Many people have told us how reading the timeline gave them the courage to face the otherwise unknown.

I want to share our **Cancer Timeline (Herman Cain)** with you:

FEBRUARY 9, 2006

During a visit to Whirlpool Headquarters in Benton Harbor, Michigan, to give a speech, a tumor in my colon that I was unaware of ruptured. I gave the speech and returned home to Atlanta that day.

FEBRUARY 10, 2006

Visit to my primary care doctor, Dr. David Vann. One of his physician assistants, John Mark, examined me and recommended I get a colonoscopy immediately.

MARCH 22, 2006

Colonoscopy performed by Dr. Brown, who confirmed that I had a tumor in my colon that was probably cancerous. The biopsy confirmed he was correct.

MARCH 29, 2006

Had a CAT scan done at Southwest Regional Medical Center.

APRIL 4, 2006

I met with a colon surgeon, Dr. Tahetia Wilson, who confirmed I had stage four cancer. When I asked what stage four is, she said, "That's as bad as it gets, because it was also in your liver." I did not know that!

APRIL 11, 2006

Got second opinion from Dr. Alan Lord (Savannah, Georgia). He confirmed all the previous results. I told him I was considering going to MD Anderson Cancer Center in Houston, Texas, for treatment. Dr. Lord said that was an excellent choice if I could get admitted. I was able to get admitted.

APRIL 24, 2006

My wife, Gloria, and I arrived at MD Anderson for orientation. It was given by the alternate at the orientation center. Her name was "Grace."

APRIL 25, 2006

Got another CAT scan done at MD Anderson this morning so Dr. Eng could review it before my afternoon appointment.

I met with Dr. Eng (oncologist), who had been assigned to my case. Her physician assistant was Fusun. They did not give a lot of last names, probably because they were so busy. But she was very nice and helpful.

Dr. Eng confirmed my diagnosis of stage four cancer. That meant it was in at least two organs of my body—in my case, in my colon and liver.

Dr. Eng recommended four chemo treatments at two-week intervals and then a rescan to see if the treatment had an effect on the tumors. If so, we could plan for surgery after a month of recovery from the chemotherapy.

APRIL 28, 2006

Met with Dr. Abdalla (surgeon) and his PA, Lee Samp. He confirmed his discussion with Dr. Eng and explained lesions on my liver affecting 80 percent of my liver.

He also explained how he removes liver sections and not just lesions.

BEST PART! Dr. Abdalla explained that the liver regenerates itself in about three months to 80 percent of original size! I DID NOT KNOW THAT! New great news!

However, having only 20 percent good liver was borderline.

He explained that colon resectioning was almost routine, no problem, and that he would remove about 30 percent of my colon and most of my liver in the same operation.

He indicated one week in the hospital after surgery, one week in Houston, and then four to six weeks recuperating at home. After which, I would need two to four weeks of chemotherapy. The length of time would depend on my progress and test results.

Sounded like a plan, I was ready to get started. Meeting with Dr. Abdalla was uplifting because he patiently explained things I did not know. I immediately felt a sense of TRUST with him and Gloria detected it also.

Dr. Abdalla thought I was in excellent physical condition and didn't see why I even had the cancer, since there was no family history with Mom, Dad, or my brother.

Sixty percent of the people who use this approach live a minimum of five years or more, and half of these are COMPLETELY CURED! "We plan for Herman to be one of the completely cured" (Gloria).

Dr. Abdalla recommended that both our children get tested by age fifty. I suggested by age forty and I would pay for the tests if necessary.

MAY 1, 2006

Dr. Abdalla's PA (Lee) called and said the CAT scan results showed that HC only had 18 percent good liver, needed minimum of 20 percent to go ahead with the surgery. He and Dr. Eng recommended that I do two months of chemo to see if the tumors on the liver would shrink to get up to the 20 percent needed.

MAY 4, 2006

Met with Dr. Martin York in Atlanta with Peachtree Chemotology to do two months of chemo (four treatments, one every other week). The plan was for the first two to be with "FOLFOX with avastin" and the second two without avastin.

Dr. Abdalla wanted the avastin out of my system before surgery since it affects blood clotting.

JULY 7, 2006

I completed the four treatments and returned to Houston for my appointment with Dr. Abdalla. The CT scan had been done the previous day. Good news! The tumors had shrunk, but the amount of good liver was still borderline. Dr. Abdalla wanted to use another procedure to make sure we were above the minimum of 20 percent good liver. He ordered a PORTAL VEIN EMBOLIZATION, never heard of it! Dr. Abdalla had me admitted to the hospital for the procedure that day. It was not an emergency, but Dr. Abdalla had the same sense of urgency I had to keep the process moving.

So, instead of being admitted for surgery at the beginning of July as we had expected, I was admitted for this special procedure, which would take another month to see the results.

Gloria and I had come prepared for a hospital stay, and I was admitted for the PVE that day, which would require at least an overnight stay.

My appointment with Dr. Abdalla started at about 9:00 A.M., and by 10:55 A.M. I was being prepped for the procedure.

After prep they took me into the surgical room at 11:10 A.M., which was to take about two and a half hours. Gloria waited in the waiting room.

A Dr. Wallace performed the PVE procedure. The procedure involved a puncture through my side into the liver to locate the veins that were to be blocked. The blocked veins would restrict blood to the bad part of the liver and allow the good part to grow faster. Simply amazing, never heard of such a thing.

At 1:10 P.M. I was out and back on the prep area where they called Gloria to come back in. I had to wait until 1:50 P.M. for a hospital room to become available.

When I woke up I did not feel any significant pain or discomfort. Taken to hospital room for overnight stay and all went well, and released the next day.

Feeling confident that the PVE would give me the cushion of good liver, Dr. Abdalla set the surgery date for August 2, 2006. A new CT scan and a meeting with Dr. Abdalla were on the preceding two days.

JULY 31, 2006

The new CT scan on July 31 showed 30 percent good liver as a result of the PVE and the prechemo! Great result!

AUGUST 1, 2006

During appointment on August 1, Dr. Abdalla very clearly explained the surgery and how it would proceed. Only one incision would be required for both the colon resectioning and the liver resectioning. I asked how and where he would cut me open. He showed me and said it would be in the shape of a "J." I immediately thought that was a good sign, a Jesus cut!

AUGUST 2, 2006, SURGERY

5:30 A.M., reported to patient registration—MD Anderson.

5:35 A.M., taken to patient prep area 5th floor.

6:40 A.M., hospital chaplain came by and did prayer with HC and GC.

7:50 A.M., Dr. Mohinda (anesthesiologist) started IV (epidural).

7:55 A.M., HC to surgery GC to waiting room with Mel and Vincent.

8:39 A.M., actual surgery started.

10:20 A.M., first update from nurse Carol. She reported everything was going well. No complications.

12:20 P.M., nurse Carol update. All the liver was done, still everything was going well. No surprises.

1:45 P.M., nurse Carol reported that the colon section had been removed, and they were reconnecting.

3:00 P.M., surgery completed! Six and half hours.

Dr. Abdalla talked with GC, Mel, and Vincent.

Took out 70 percent of liver, 30 percent left to grow back.

Took all lymph nodes out (about forty-eight). Saw no surprises.

Removed one-third of colon and fused remaining sections.

"He has a lot of healing to do, but expect HC to do well."

No blood transfusion needed, minimal bleeding.

"Dr. Abdalla said from his experience 50 percent of patients have tumors to grow back. If so, we will deal with it. But the fact that the chemo worked before surgery was a good sign. We would use the same chemo postsurgery."

5:00 P.M., HC still in recovery but GC (my blessing) was able to see me for ten minutes. When I woke up tubes were coming out of me everywhere. Nose, penis, side, both arms. It was uncomfortable but I kept telling myself it was a blessing to be alive and able to have such a difficult surgery with a most capable surgeon.

Later on I was able to see Mel and Vincent for few minutes.

Next day I was moved to a hospital room. GC had arrived early while I was still in recovery. Dr. Abdalla wanted me to try to start walking around right away to help stimulate systems restart. All I could eat was ice chips for a while. Hospital stay was originally supposed to be a week, but it turned into three weeks. My digestive system was slow to restart, and Dr. Abdalla did not want to release me until it had. Many tests were run to see if there were blockages or complications but there were NONE.

Those three weeks were very trying because a lot could have gone wrong but it didn't by God's grace. *Finally,* my systems started to respond, but I had to start eating more. When I could not I was put on IV nutrition, which helped, which I stayed on well into my recovery at home.

It turned out that the heavy pain medication they gave me in the hospital was slowing down my systems. When I started taking Motrin instead of the strong intravenous stuff, things started coming back. Hallelujah!

AUGUST 24, 2006 (THURSDAY), RELEASED FROM HOSPITAL

We stayed in the Rotary House Hotel for a week before returning home to Atlanta. After three weeks in the hospital instead of one I was so ready to go home, but I knew I could not go home too soon.

AUGUST 28, 2006 (MONDAY)

Our best friends Gladys and Joel Ricks had come to Houston the day before my surgery, and stayed in Houston until Gloria and I returned to Atlanta. We did not ask them to do that, but Gladys and Gloria are closer than sisters and they were there for her and me. What a true blessing. They had driven to Houston and headed back to Atlanta two days before Gloria and I headed home by plane.

AUGUST 29, 2006 (TUESDAY)

I had a follow-up visit with Dr. Abdalla. I also met with a nutritionist, who instructed me to keep track of my calorie intake. Stay on TPN until calories reach about two thousand per day or more from eating food, and then gradually get off TPN. I forgot what TPN stands for, but it's that intravenous nutrition I had to take through my arm. In a few weeks I was able to eat two thousand calories a day because I was sick of that intravenous stuff.

Dr. Abdalla told me to call his PA (Lee) once a week with updates on recovery. If anything unusual persisted I was to let them know. Thankfully, the recovery went as expected.

SEPTEMBER 1, 2006 (FRIDAY)

Gloria and I flew back to Atlanta! Fortunately, one of the boards I serve on as a director sent their company plane to bring us home. This was particularly helpful in that I was still not feeling very strong, and we did not have to endure the stress of commercial travel. Without the company plane we would have stayed in Houston about a week longer. I do not want to identify the company because some jackass might want to make an issue out of it. We are very thankful for the gesture.

I felt bad and weak but was determined to get home. I was able to get dressed and packed and we made it.

Joel and Gladys picked us up at the airport when we got to Atlanta. I told you they were special!

HOME AGAIN!

American Home Care provided TPN and periodic blood tests. Gloria became a great in-home "nurse," staying on top of vitals and what I was supposed to do. She also became proficient at changing the bandages on my TPN line, and connecting the TPN nightly. I don't think that's in the marriage vows, but that's what love looks like.

I ate aggressively so I could get off the TPN. I accomplished that goal in about three weeks, and continued to recover.

OCTOBER 10, 2006

I had my first follow-up visit with Dr. Abdalla and Dr. Eng in Houston. I had another CT scan and all systems looked good! I was now ready to start postsurgery chemo. They recommended six treatments.

OCTOBER 13, 2006

I met with Dr. York. His nurse removed the PIC line for TPN, because I was now eating enough calories per day. We scheduled all six chemo treatments to restart on October 23 and continue through January 3, 2007, every other week.

Gloria went with me for the first two treatments, because she wanted to know exactly what was going on as she had done throughout the surgery and recovery. It was about a four-and-a-half-hour process each time and it was nice to have her there with me. Joel offered to take me the last four times, and we accepted, to give Gloria a break. Did I mention that Gloria went through all of this with me with a threatening heart condition? Joel's assistance helped both of us.

JANUARY 3, 2007, LAST CHEMO TREATMENT!

After each chemo treatment I would also have a pump attached, which would continue to inject chemotherapy into my system for two days. I would return to be disconnected from the pump until my next treatment. My last disconnect was on January 5, 2007!

I do not know what it feels like to get out of jail, but this was the most liberating experience of my life. I was not even focused on whether it all worked or not, because I knew the doctors had done all they could do, and I had done all I could do. That was God's plan and all was in His hands.

NEW YEAR! NEW DAY! NEW OUTLOOK FOR 2007 AND BEYOND!

8

The Call to Serve

*If my people which are called by my name, shall humble
themselves, and pray, and seek my face, and turn from
their wicked ways; then I will hear from heaven, and
forgive their sin, and will heal their land.*
                                        —2 Chronicles 7:14

I've been a prayerful man and faithful church participant
since childhood. And both in our home and when dining
out, before I break bread, whether with family and friends or
in business meetings, I always say the following grace: "Father,
we thank you for this food for the nourishment of our bodies.
And Lord, we thank you for this day and this fellowship. And
Lord, we ask that you continue to give us strength to do the
things that Thou would have us do, not our will. Amen."

Given that I'm also a strong believer in using my God-
given talents, I was convinced in 2006, after having van-

quished life-threatening stage four cancer, that I could help to rally the voice of "we the people," which had been hijacked by partisan politics, government bureaucrats, and the influence of money on elections and legislation.

While my having survived cancer against the odds was a major tipping point in my decision to seek the Republican Party's presidential nomination in 2012, I first realized my need and responsibility to do so many years earlier, actually a few minutes before ten o'clock on the evening of January 22, 1999.

That was when I held my first-born grandchild, Celena, in my arms only moments after her birth. I'll never forget that moment. As I looked at her beautiful little face, I realized that I needed to move beyond the corporate world to the political arena and use my time and the talent I've been blessed with by God to help make this a better world for *her* sake, and for all the other little faces.

While you've just read some serious stuff, the timing of Celena's arrival was not without its humorous aspect. I wasn't supposed to get back from a business trip out of town in time to be there for the blessed event—but *I did*, and my first granddaughter was born only minutes after my arrival at the hospital.

The labor had already been going on for three days. I kept calling home and the hospital, asking my son, "Do we have a baby yet?"

"No, Dad, we don't have a baby yet."

Day two: "Has the baby been born?"

"No, Dad. The baby hasn't been born."

Day three: I was on my way back to Atlanta and I was supposed to arrive in the evening. I called Vincent when I landed at the airport: "Vincent, do we have a baby yet?"

"No, Dad. We don't have a baby yet!"

"Is Melanie okay?"

"Yes!"

"Are there any complications?"

"No."

"Why don't we have a *baby* yet?"

"Dad, it's a *s-l-o-w* baby."

"I know that."

I landed in Atlanta at about 8:30 P.M. At 9:30 P.M. I was at the hospital, up in the waiting area, near the delivery area. I went in and sat down. Vincent was there.

I said, "Vincent, do we have a baby yet?"

"No, we don't have a baby yet, Dad."

At 9:56 P.M. my wife came out of the delivery room with her hands on her hips, moving that neck—man, you know you're in a heap of trouble when the neck is moving and the hands are on the hips. She didn't even say, "Hello, honey. I'm glad you made it back all the way from Hawaii to Atlanta safely." Her first words were, "You have a granddaughter!"

I said, "Wonderful! Is Melanie okay?"

"Yes."

"Is the baby all right?"

"Yes."

"Then what's with the *attitude*?"

She said, "I've been with this girl for three days, and you show up and the baby is born!"

"She was waiting on Granddad."

"I *know* she was waiting on Granddaddy," she said. "I'm going to have to hear that story for the rest of my life: 'She was waiting for Granddad to come into this world!' "

I went into the delivery room and saw my daughter and said, "Melanie, are you okay?"

"Yes."

"Is the baby okay?"

"Yes," she said. "Would you like to hold her?"

"Of course," I said.

My first grandchild! I didn't think: How do I give her a good start in life? How do I make sure she gets a good education? The first thought that went through my mind was: What do *I* do to make this a better world and a better nation?

I was so moved as I held my precious first-born grandchild in my arms that I was inspired to write the following verse, which I signed as The Hermanator, aka Herman Cain:

LITTLE FACES

As she lay there in her mother's arms,
She was only a few minutes old.
My baby daughter had just had a baby girl,
A precious new member of a great big world.

My baby daughter said, "Would you like to hold her?"
Of course I said yes, as my smile grew bolder.
As I picked her up with a gentle touch,
She was small, so fragile, and yet so much.

She had gone back to sleep after the struggle to start her life.
Baby and Mommy were fine, everything was all right.
When I looked at that little face, sent from God above,
It was truly the face of a miracle, and of God's divine love.

For a moment, I didn't know who I was or where,
I could only think of her and so happy to be there.
Born into the world with all the other little faces,
What will we do, to make it a better place?

I know that came from God Almighty, and I've been on a twelve-year journey ever since, trying to figure out what I'm supposed to do in order to help make this a better world, and to make America a better country again. And I know that we live in the greatest country in the world, even though the current occupant of the White House doesn't understand that concept. He doesn't think that America is exceptional, but most of us think that it *is*.

I've been campaigning for many months now, talking to a lot of people and listening to them. And I've got to tell you: Their disconnect from this president and this administration is absolutely *unbelievable*.

But come November 6, 2012, there will be a reconnect; a very different kind of commander in chief—a CEO of Self—will be elected, one who knows how to make the United States of America united again.

Herman Cain at age five.
REPRINTED BY PERMISSION OF
THE ESTATE OF LENORA CAIN

Luther Cain, Herman's beloved father and mentor, Atlanta, Georgia, 1970. REPRINTED BY PERMISSION OF THE ESTATE OF LENORA CAIN

Herman Cain as a senior at Archer High School in Atlanta, Georgia, 1963. Voted "Most Likely to Succeed." REPRINTED BY PERMISSION OF ATLANTA PUBLIC SCHOOLS

Most Likely To Succeed
HERMAN CAIN and MARTHA JONES

Herman Cain as a student at Morehouse College in Atlanta, Georgia, 1966. REPRINTED BY PERMISSION OF THE ESTATE OF LENORA CAIN

Herman and Gloria Cain on their wedding day, June 23, 1968. From left to right: Gloria's uncle, Herbert Thompson; Gloria's mother, Mrs. Lula Milligan; Gloria; Herman; Herman's mother, Lenora Cain; and father, Luther Cain. REPRINTED BY PERMISSION OF THE ESTATE OF LENORA CAIN

Herman Cain enjoying a vacation at Disney World in 1971.
COURTESY OF GLORIA CAIN

Herman Cain receiving his Honorary Doctorate in Science degree from Purdue University on December 19, 2004. REPRINTED BY PERMISSION OF PURDUE UNIVERSITY

From left to right: Gloria; Herman; son, Vincent; and daughter, Melanie, in 1993 at the Ak-Sar-Ben Aksarben Foundation Coronation Ball in Omaha, Nebraska. REPRINTED BY PERMISSION OF THE KNIGHTS OF AK-SAR-BEN FOUNDATION, OMAHA, NEBRASKA

Herman Cain in the sanctuary of Antioch Baptist Church, North,
Atlanta, Georgia, March 2011. REPRINTED BY PERMISSION OF FRIENDS OF
HERMAN CAIN

Herman Cain doing his radio show in his office in Stockbridge, Georgia, January 2010. COURTESY OF MELANIE CAIN JACKSON

Herman Cain speaking to the tax reform group Americans for Prosperity in March 2010. REPRINTED BY PERMISSION OF MARK BLOCK

Crowd at Centennial Olympic Park, on presidential announcement day, May 21, 2011. COURTESY OF LEE SHIFLETT

Herman Cain announces his bid for the Republican nomination for president of the United States at Centennial Olympic Park in his hometown of Atlanta on May 21, 2011. COURTESY OF LEE SHIFLETT

Herman Cain and his entire family take the stage at Centennial Olympic Park on announcement day. From left to right: grandson Preston Jackson, age 7; daughter, Melanie Cain-Jackson; daughter-in-law, Karol Cain; granddaughter, Celena Jackson, age 12; son, Vincent, holding grandson Ryan, age 18 months; wife, Gloria; and Herman Cain. COURTESY OF RICHARD NORRIS

Presidential candidate Herman Cain in his favorite black hat, Atlanta, Georgia, March 3, 2011. REPRINTED BY PERMISSION OF FRIENDS OF HERMAN CAIN

9

"Forty-five"— A Special Number

And this is the confidence that we have in Him, that, if
we ask any thing according to His will, He heareth us.

—1 John, 5:14

People often attach great significance to a particular number because they believe that it has had, or is continuing to
have, a particular impact on their lives.

In my case, that number is 45. And given that I was born
on December 13, 1945—my conception, gestation, and birth
all occurred within that year—that number has been with me,
literally, for all my life, to date.

The number 45 keeps on popping up as I go about the business of being elected—you guessed it—as the forty-fifth president of the United States of America.

There was actually one instance, in March 2010, where Mark Block and Linda Hansen, the executive vice president and deputy chief of staff of my campaign, had mistakenly thought that 45 had surfaced again. We were sitting at a table in the Capital Grille in Las Vegas having a decisive meeting and both Mark and Linda thought we were sitting at Table 45, but we were not. It turned out to be Table 5.

It turns out that the Capital Grille's highest-numbered table is only 43. But not to worry: As you will learn shortly, we would get to enjoy the opportunity of dining at a table with that very meaningful number.

As the November 2010 elections neared, Mark, Linda, and I were becoming more and more aware of how often 45 was popping up on the scene. For example, I was participating at that time in an Americans for Prosperity bus tour in Florida when the driver, whose name was Johnny, said that he had told his brother about me.

It turned out that Johnny's brother had seen me on Fox News and knew that I was planning to run for president, so he sent Johnny an article for me to read that had been published many years earlier by the *Reader's Digest*. It contained introductory notes and the condensed version of the Austrian-born economist Friedrich A. von Hayek's milestone and controversial book, *The Road to Serfdom*, first published in 1944 in Britain.

Dr. Hayek—who had earned two Ph.D.s from the University of Vienna, in law and political economy, and later became a professor at both the London School of Economics and the University of Chicago—expressed his belief in that article that America was facing a socialist takeover.

That's exactly what people are saying about where the United States of America is today—that we are actually on the brink of a totally socialist takeover. I and others of my political persuasion believe that Barack Obama is fundamentally a socialist because we believe he simply does not understand the free-market system. And I fear that if he were to be re-elected in 2012, Dr. Hayek's prediction of the 1940s could become the harsh reality of the twenty-first century.

Dr. Hayek also wrote: "I advocate that we press in the direction of individual freedom, and the concomitant responsibilities to ourselves, our posterity, and the preservation of the Nation and the Constitution for the United States."

Doesn't that sound familiar?

Dr. Hayek predicted that the government could get too big and spending could go out of control. Isn't that exactly where we are today?

What was the year of the *Reader's Digest* article's publication?

Nineteen forty-five, of course!

While it was weird in itself for Johnny's brother to have sent him that article to put in my hands, what happened later that week, when I was in Cleveland to give a speech, was even weirder. Mark Block and I decided to have dinner in the restaurant of the hotel where we were staying. And what do you think the name of that restaurant was?

Table 45, of course!

When we asked the chef how the restaurant had come by

its name, he told us that in the establishment where he had previously worked, private parties were often accommodated at a table in the kitchen designated *Number 45.*

Now let's look at another instance of how that special number has followed me wherever I go. It's a long story, but here's the short version: In April 2011, during an eight-day period that Mark and I would come to call our "Hell Week" because everything was going wrong—so much so that I was even considering ending my campaign—we were on a crucial swing through several states and we faced more logistical challenges than I would wish on any opponent, among them chartered aircraft too small to accommodate two tall guys.

On the final leg of that trip from hell—we were going home to Atlanta after having traveled through parts of six states—our flight number was 1045. And if that wasn't coincidence enough, on another flight—we were traveling in a private aircraft—when I asked Mark to find out from the pilot what altitude we were flying at, his answer was, "Forty-five thousand feet."

Several weeks later, on the evening of Wednesday, May 18, 2011, I was speaking to a group of several hundred people at the Standard at the Smith House, in Nashville, Tennessee, and my message must really have been resonating because they kept interrupting what I was saying with applause and cheers.

Why?

Maybe it's because I said things like, "When I started doing a radio show in Atlanta, it forced me to learn more about the problems and the solutions we face than I ever wanted to know, because, as you know and I know, 50 percent of the American public are clueless as to what's going on. And that simply means that the rest of us have to work harder to get smarter people to the polls to basically outvote those that are clueless. And I happen to believe that we will be able to do that."

Maybe it's because I referred to Obamacare as the president's "health care deform bill," or because I said, "I, like you, I could not sit back and watch the president and his administration intentionally destroy the greatest nation in the world." Or because I asked a rhetorical question: "When was the last time they fixed something in Washington, D.C.?" and answered, "The Revolutionary War may have been the last time they did that!" And maybe it's because I told them, "As a businessman, I'd use the same approach to problem-solving that I have used to become successful."

Or maybe it was because, after asking the crowd, "Remember when the president joked during a discussion about illegal immigration: 'What do the Republicans want? Do they want a moat, with alligators?' I said to the crowd, 'Yes! Bring on the alligators! And make it a *real big* moat!' "

Maybe it's because I told the crowd that when I heard a liberal reporter say, "That's so uncompassionate," I said, "I don't think it's uncompassionate. If they can get into the moat and get over my fence, which is going to be twenty feet high, and they can outswim the alligators, I'd give them a job! It wasn't compassionate when they killed some of our agents on the borders. It's not compassionate when they kill ranchers on the border. It's not compassionate when you sue Arizona! They ought to be giving Arizona a prize! Stay tuned for 'Herman's Moat.'"

I always welcome that kind of interruption, but I was astounded a few days later, when one of the people traveling with my campaign that week who had witnessed those interruptions emailed Mark: "Do you know how many times Mr. Cain's speech was actually interrupted with applause? Forty-five times!"

I kid you not.

Then on Sunday, June 12, 2011, I was writing my weekly commentary, entitled "Watch and Hope Won't Work"—now they're saying the economy is going to get better, but it's *not* going to get better—and when I checked the number of words, I discovered that it came to 645!

Now, as I was writing my commentary, I didn't say: I'm going to hit 645. It just turned out to be 645 words and I said, "Mark, this is it! I'm not changing a word!"

More recently, in July 2011, when I was in Las Vegas to deliver a speech at the Conservative Leadership Conference, a couple came up to me when I was walking through a hotel lobby and said that they recognized me, that they knew I was running for president. Then they told me why they were in Las Vegas. They were there to celebrate their forty-fifth wedding anniversary!

That isn't all: Next year will be the forty-fifth anniversary of my college graduation. And in 2013, my first year in the White House, Gloria and I will be celebrating our forty-fifth wedding anniversary.

I'm not a devout numerologist, but my mathematical training does cause me to recognize when numbers appear more than coincidentally.

Isn't it amazing how often 45 keeps popping up in my life?

10

The Cain Doctrine

I have set the LORD always before me: for he is at my
right hand, I shall not be moved.

—Psalm 16:8

As any student of American history knows, in the nineteenth century we had the Monroe Doctrine, because our new nation's fifth president found it necessary to warn European powers not to intervene in the Western Hemisphere.

In the twentieth century we had the Truman Doctrine, because our thirty-third president was so alarmed at cold war aggression that he found it necessary to declare the United States' support of people throughout the world who were resisting armed oppressors.

Now in the twenty-first century, after having given much thought to identifying the crucial domestic and foreign policy issues of this era and developing what is, essentially, a common sense approach to fixing the mess besetting this great nation of ours, the time has come for me, as the forty-fifth commander in chief, to enunciate to the American people my doctrine: the Cain Doctrine.

Unlike its predecessor doctrines, which dealt solely with demanding that foreign powers keep their hands off places where they had no business being, the Cain Doctrine also takes on the critical domestic issues of today and provides my scenario for righting the lapses of the Obama administration. These lapses, if not resolved, will continue to threaten both our great nation's economic future and international security.

The domestic issues section of the Cain Doctrine grew out of my experience in the corporate world, where I learned about the impact of taxes on business and on individuals. That's when I started to figure out that the Democrats wanted to tax you and regulate you and the Republicans wanted to lower taxes and reduce regulations.

Before that, I was like everybody else: You don't know what your ideology is; you just get an impression of a candidate over the course of a campaign and you say, "I like this person so I'm going to vote for him." And I did the same thing: I liked Ronald Reagan, so I voted for him. But I never got deeply into politics.

It was only when I became president of Godfather's Pizza, Inc., that I really started to pay attention. Now, as I campaign for the Republican Party's presidential nomination, my Domestic Cain Doctrine is as follows:

Energy: I would never go to a foreign country, loan them money, and then tell them we'll be their best customer. Under provisions of the Cain Doctrine, we, America, will be *our own* best customer.

Immigration: It must occur legally, through the front door, not the side door or the back door. And as for the underlying, acute problem—the illegal entrants themselves—the way to deal with them is to do what the federal government can't, or won't, do: empower the states to resolve their individual situations. In other words: Don't sue Arizona—award that state a prize!

But one of the basic reasons for Washington's inability to deal with illegal immigration, as with so many other problems, is the federal government's inability to micromanage anything. I defy anybody to come up with one example of successful federal micromanaging.

The good news is that I have a plan: Secure our borders—remember that deep moat? Enforce laws already on the books and facilitate the path to citizenship. We don't need a new path, one is already in place. We should recognize that there are no so-called undocumented workers in this country—these people are here *illegally*. After all, have you ever heard anyone say, "I'm an undocumented bank robber?"

Abortion: While I view abortion in the gravest possible moral and ethical terms and I want to defund Planned Parenthood, there is confusion about where I stand on the issue. I can say with certainty that I am prolife, although certain sectors of the public and the media don't think that I am. And that's likely because when the Susan B. Anthony Association asked all presidential candidates to sign their 2012 Pro-Life Presidential Leadership Pledge, I did not agree to do so.

Why not, given my prolife stance?

Because when I received the text of the pledge, I did something that most people don't do: I actually read it! And I even agreed with everything in it, that is, except for the last requirement, which concerns a proposed "Pain-Capable Unborn Child Protection Act."

While I could favor the act itself, with further clarification, there is one word in the pledge related to it that I could never agree to because signers are called upon to "advance" that particular piece of legislation. As president, I simply would not have the constitutional power to act in that manner. I would be able to support, but not *advance* legislation. Thus I simply could not sign on to something that violates my understanding of the powers inherent in the presidency.

And I wasn't going to sign the pledge just to avoid negative publicity. I don't want to promise things that I cannot do. Of course, if the Susan B. Anthony Association had been willing to change the word "advance" to "support," I would gladly have been on board.

While my stand on the matter did engender some negative comments, when I spoke at the National Right to Life convention a few days after the issue erupted, I received several standing ovations. And that's because the delegates did not have a problem with my not signing the pledge. They knew my position on the right to life issue. They knew that I am prolife.

Now, as for the Cain Doctrine's position on the most crucial and troubling issue challenging America's well-being today, the economy, we must pursue a two-phase approach.

Phase One, in four parts: First, lower tax rates, both corporate and personal—we're the only country in the world that has not lowered its top corporate tax rate in fifteen years—and I would go with the recommendation in Paul Ryan's plan; take the top corporate tax rate from 35 percent to 25 percent and lower the top personal income tax rate as well.

Second, take the capital gains tax to zero—that will help to stimulate the generation of cash for small businesses.

Third, suspend taxes on repatriated foreign profits; we've got nearly $3 trillion that have been generated by multinational corporations and the money is offshore. And if we suspend taxes on it, much of it will come back home. When Bush did this in 2003, nearly $350 billion came back into this economy. It's now estimated that as much as $3 trillion could come back, according to Eric Bolling of Fox Business News.

Fourth, give a real payroll tax holiday to workers, as well as to the employers; instead of that piddling 2 percent that the administration and Congress passed at the end of 2010, do the full 6.2 percent for a year for the employees and the employers.

Then put a bow around these ideas—that is, with the exception of the payroll tax—and make them permanent. That's called an "Economic Boost"—in other words, America's economy takes off when you allow workers and businesses to keep more of the money they generate, rather than raising taxes and then going through that government filter, which doesn't give anything back to the public and doesn't stimulate the economy.

Phase Two: Replace the entire tax code with the Fair Tax. I've had a lot of feedback from folks: "That can't be done. It's too difficult." My answer to them is: "If you think that way, you don't know much about Herman Cain. I don't avoid doing something because it's going to be hard to do it. I do it because it is the right thing to do."

But I do understand people's reservations concerning the Fair Tax, and that's why I would not attempt to pass the necessary legislation in my first two years in office. For now, we've got to educate more people and counter the demagoguery that goes out there whenever I talk about the Fair Tax.

With Phase One and Phase Two, we could supercharge this economy, and we won't even have to look back at China, which right now is gaining on us.

We need to take these bold steps to get this economy moving again and not the small steps that President Obama and some of the other Democrats keep talking about.

The revolving door resignation of at least four of President Obama's senior economic advisers is a prime example of the fact that his administration lacks real leadership. And the problem did not lie with the advisers, but with President Obama. It's *his* problem, because he has not developed sound economic policy, so it doesn't matter who he appoints to senior positions.

We have the capacity to grow this economy a lot more than it's growing, but we simply don't have the leadership to get it done. I happen to believe that that's what we need to do. And, more important, I believe that we can *do* it.

Social Security, Medicare, and Medicaid: We can, and we must, take this entitlement society to an empowerment society. When I talk about really being serious about cutting costs, some people say to me: "You just can't do that!"

Why not? Some people told me I couldn't survive cancer, but I did! Other people said I couldn't turn Godfather's Pizza, Inc., around, but it's still going! Okay, I admit I can't break 80 on a golf course, but you've got to understand that I'm not perfect.

Foreign policy issues: My critics claim that I have had no "hands on" foreign policy experience, having been a mere business leader these many decades.

Well, I may not have been around Washington all these years to help those insiders deal with all of the complexities of the dangerous world we live in, but I can declare with certainty that I know enough about the importance of supporting one's allies, especially in this age of international terrorism and despotism, to know that you don't throw your faithful friends under the bus.

I'm referring to Israel, and I can tell you what the Cain Doctrine would be: If you mess with Israel, you're messing with the United States of America. Is that clear?

I've been following the situation in the Middle East for decades now and I was shocked that on May 19, 2011, President Obama wrongheadedly betrayed America's most steadfast ally in that region with his arrogant demand for the sovereign nation's return to its pre-1967 Six Day War borders.

First of all, a move like that would threaten Israel's security; embolden those countries in the Middle East that are trying to intimidate Israel into just going away. It would also destabilize the whole region.

Second, Israel is an ally of ours, and if some major conflict were to break out in that part of the world, we would need its assistance militarily, in terms of being a conduit for supplies, fuel, and other combat-related resources. And if it ever came to pass that the great relationship we now have with Israel was eroded, not only would our staunch ally become very vulnerable, but we would lose our capability in the entire Middle East. Even worse, America's reputation for supporting its friends would be gone.

So should the Obama administration do everything in its power to maintain and nurture our great relationship with Israel?

My answer is an unequivocal "Yes!"

But is the Obama administration doing that?

My response is an emphatic "No!"

And that's not what we the people want. I can tell you that everywhere I go as I campaign for my party's presidential nomination, people are still in shock over President Obama's demand for Israel to revert to its 1967 borders.

Why?

Because, like me, they are unabashedly pro-Israel.

For instance, on Friday, May 20, 2011, the day after President Obama's ultimatum to Israel, I was in Council Bluffs, Iowa, speaking at the Pottawattamie County Republican Party's annual Lincoln Reagan Day Dinner, and every time I mentioned my support for Israel, the attendees stood up and cheered and applauded.

So why doesn't *President Obama* get it?

Why doesn't he realize the strategic nature of Israel's current borders and that their inward movement would enable Israel's enemies to lob weapons at them, as they did from Lebanon several years ago.

And why is this president not aware of another bad thing resulting from what he has done to Israel, namely that our other allies around the world are now wondering: How can we trust *this* president and *this* administration, when America's most loyal friend in the Middle East has been thrown under the bus?

It's difficult to say how the Cain Doctrine would apply to the Middle East's other countries, especially those affected by the "Arab Spring," and to nations elsewhere in the world. I'm not trying to escape the broader issues, but I think a president should first be briefed on classified intelligence about America's relationships before offering opinions.

The public doesn't know the answers to those questions and neither do I. Do I want to get out of Afghanistan? Yes. The only question is *when*. The two biggest mistakes we can make in Afghanistan are (1) to leave too soon if we can win, and (2) to stay too long if we can't win. My plan would be to figure out: Can we win, or not?

The media doesn't like that answer. But the public loves that answer because it's honest. There's more that I don't know than I do know.

What I do know is that I would clarify our mission and our ability to prevail in a given situation. That would mean asking the right questions and figuring out policy based on information about those nations' weapons capabilities, because it's not just about bombs and bullets; it's about bombs, bullets, and free enterprise and economics.

Another area where the media just doesn't like what I have to say is on the thorny issue of Sharia law. The purveyors of political correctness want us to let down our guard on issues like that so that they can seep into American life.

As a knowledgeable friend of mine has pointed out, the United States is based on a written Constitution, while Islam is a religious-political ideology. I suggest that people read Tony Blankley's *The West's Last Chance*. In it he tells how Europe has become conflicted because of the gradual infusion over time of Islam's religious and political system, and that some European nations are having a difficult time making rulings as to when to apply Sharia law and when to apply the existing laws.

Our country simply wasn't set up that way. We need to keep in mind that it was radical Islamists who murdered almost three thousand people on 9/11, tried to blow up Times Square, and committed the Fort Hood massacre. I don't apologize for the way I feel.

So the Cain Doctrine on that one is: The United States of America will not invoke Sharia law—at least not on my watch.

American laws in American courts.

11

Post–High Noon
at Centennial Olympic Park

Trust in the LORD with all thine heart; and lean
not unto thine own understanding. In all thy ways
acknowledge Him, and He will direct thy paths.

—Proverbs 3:5–6

I don't think that too many people were surprised when on Saturday, May 21, 2011, I formally announced my candidacy before an audience of fifteen thousand at Centennial Olympic Park in my hometown, Atlanta.

After all, more than a year earlier, in April 2010, I had teased the audience at the Southern Republican Leadership Conference with my reference to a dark horse candidate for our party's 2012 presidential nomination.

Later, on September 24, 2010, I went a step further, announcing that I was actually considering seeking the party's nomination. That was when things really took off: In December, in a reader poll conducted on the conservative website RedState.com, I was the surprise choice for the party's presidential nomination, edging out the former vice presidential candidate and governor of Alaska Sarah Palin. The *National Review*'s Jonah Goldberg weighed in at that time, writing: "It's hard to imagine him amounting to more than an exciting also-ran."

But media negativity doesn't intimidate Herman Cain. I decided that the time was right to form a presidential exploratory committee, and I announced my intention to do so on January 12, 2011, during the Fox News Channel's program *Your World with Neil Cavuto*.

That declaration provoked even more media negativity. Jonah Goldberg's observation had been positively benign compared to the brutality and racism of the news website AlterNet, which accused me of pandering to white conservatives. To drive that point home, I and my fellow black conservatives were described as being "garbage pail kids." That playing of the race card was shameful!

But there was positive feedback, too. Ed Morrissey, writing on the conservative website Hot Air of my appearance at the Conservative Political Action Conference (CPAC), in February 2011, reported that I "stole the show" and that my speech had moved some of the attendees to tears.

Among those attendees was a prominent Tennessean who had introduced himself to me following my speech. On May 18 he introduced me at the meeting at the Standard at the Smith House, in Nashville. He reminded me then of his having experienced a "God moment" when I spoke at the CPAC meeting.

This man had gone to Washington because, in his words, "I wanted to hear what the potential presidential candidates had to say, and I wanted to hear it firsthand. I didn't want it watered down by the press."

He said that while he had heard some very good speakers, he had also heard some whose underlying aim was to talk about all the accolades they had received and all the things they had accomplished as our representatives. That gave him pause. He was thinking, "Wait a minute. Look at the direction that the country is going. It's hard for me to recognize the way it was just a few short years ago. We have more problems today than you can imagine and you're standing up there, telling me how great you are and I'm wondering: Why you don't take some personal responsibility for the mess that we're in?"

Then, he said, "I heard Herman Cain. He said some of the same things that I heard from the others, but it came from his heart and his soul and I believed every word he said. He talked about some of the problems that we face, but he also talked about some of the solutions to those problems." He had never heard such talk before from any other potential candidate—that what I said took him "on such an emotional roller coaster ride."

When I got through speaking, he said, "I've got to go down and tell Herman Cain how I feel." But to get down to where I was standing, he had to get through the crowd of people I was already talking with, and he thought I would get offstage before he got there.

I don't like to rush off without talking to the people who have come out to hear what I have to say, so when he approached me, I listened to what he had to say—his "God moment." He said to me, "You're the real deal, and if there's anything I can ever do for you, please don't hesitate to call me."

Then he walked away, thinking he would never hear from me. What he didn't realize at that moment was that if I say to someone, "I'm going to give you a call," I make that call. So he did hear from me again. On May 18 when this man introduced me to that crowd in Nashville, he said, "Well, ladies and gentlemen, you're looking at another 'God moment.' I want you to meet the next president of the United States."

"This is a 'God moment' for me, too," I told him.

Getting back to my decision to make a run for my party's 2012 presidential nomination: In addition to stirring both those who welcomed what I had to say and those who didn't—actually, most people were thinking, "Herman Cain's not going to win because he's never held public office before, and you've got to have a certain amount of money"—my declaration of intent also had repercussions within my immediate family. While Melanie and Vincent were fine with it, observing, "That's just Dad being *Dad*," Gloria didn't immediately jump up and down and cheer.

In fact, she was terrified! Scared to death! That was because of the widely held perception of what it's like to be in politics—of what it can do to your family and to *you*, the candidate. While Gloria had, of course, been through my run for the Senate in 2004, that was not as big a deal.

Incidentally, that race was very helpful in terms of lessons learned. I learned that if I were ever to run for public office again, I would have to start early. I was a year late in putting together an effective team. I also learned that I would need to hire good people early on, and that even though there were very few black Republicans in most of Georgia's 159 counties, when people listened to my message, it was not about the color of my skin. I knew that if I could win that kind of reaction from rural Georgia, I would not need to worry about responses in the rest of the country. I learned that in today's America, it's not about color. It's about the content of your ideas. It's about your passion.

But when I started talking about running for president? *That* was a big deal.

I wanted to reassure Gloria about what I had just committed to doing, so I asked her, "What's your greatest fear about my running?"

"That you might win!" she answered.

"Is that all there is?" I asked.

"No," she said. "I've seen you do the impossible before, by the grace of God."

I didn't give Gloria a speech about all the reasons why I wanted to run, because that wouldn't have made a difference to her. She came around after I took her to a number of fundraising events. While I don't insist that she go to a lot of them, she's been to about three now, and she sees the enthusiasm of the people, especially when I tell them *why* I'm running: that it's for the kids and the grandkids. Gloria loves those grandkids dearly, and that resonates with her more than my trying to sit down at the breakfast table and explain why I'm running. And she knows that I believe in my heart that God is in this journey.

My first step after announcing my candidacy was to assemble my campaign team. I'd known Mark Block, who had been a leader in the Tea Party movement in Wisconsin, for several years. After his appointment six years ago as the Wisconsin state director of Americans for Prosperity, the organization's president asked me to help them launch some state chapters, so Mark brought me in for an eight-stop, day-and-a-half trip through the state.

Our foray was so exhausting that at its end, when I got back to the airport for my return trip to Atlanta, I called one of Americans for Prosperity's directors and asked, "Is this Block guy trying to *kill* me?"

But I forgave Mark, and during the next six months, when Mark was asked to launch branches in Michigan and Ohio and I was asked to help him, I agreed to do so and we ended up spending a lot of time together, much of it in a car, traveling from meeting to meeting.

On one of those occasions, Mark had scheduled a meeting in rural Michigan and only one person showed up. But to me, it was as if five thousand people were in that room. And later on, when Mark organized what were called "Defending the American Dream Summits," I was always a speaker.

As I got to know Mark better, I was impressed that not only was he a tireless worker as we traveled the state making appearances on behalf of the movement, but even though he has been in politics for most of his professional life, he is truly blessed with the *sine qua non* of the professional campaign chief of staff: the talent for thinking out of the box. In my case, thinking *way* out of that box. And that's one of the reasons we have a great relationship.

Then, when I talked to him about my running for the presidency, I said, "Mark, we can't do this top-down. I don't have that kind of money."

"I don't think we have to," he said.

"Why not?" I wanted to know.

"Because I've heard you speak many, many, many times. No one can match you in your ability to move a crowd. You will have an advantage coming out of the gate. You don't need a top-down. You need a bottom-up!"

And so Mark signed on to run my campaign. We set up our headquarters in a suburb of Atlanta, began to put together an unconventional campaign, and set about recruiting our unconventional staff. Nobody was more unconventional than Mark Block. One day, when he was taking out the garbage, he was getting off the elevator when another staff person was getting on with a VIP. On Mark's return to his office a few minutes later, the staff member escorted the VIP in. And when Mark was introduced as my chief of staff, the VIP asked him, "But aren't you the guy who just took out the garbage?"

"When you work with Mr. Cain, getting the job done has no boundaries," Mark replied.

As we moved along to increase our visibility, one of our biggest challenges was to find people to work with us who understood what we were trying to do—staff members who were able to fit into our more than a bit out-of-the-box campaign culture. Not only did we succeed in doing so, we created a new paradigm and changed the way politics is done in America.

Among our think-out-of-the-box strategists is Mark's number two, Linda Hansen, who home-schooled her six children and worked with Mark in Wisconsin. Linda and I actually met at an Americans for Prosperity event there, and I was impressed with the concept of a project she was working on, a book and program entitled *Prosperity 101*.™

When Linda—Mark and I address her simply as "Hansen"—first told me of her project, which was aimed at educating employers to teach their employees about issues affecting their jobs, and to which I ended up contributing a few pages, I responded that it was "a capitalist response to Acorn." I added, "I'm on the radio and people don't need Prosperity 101. They need Prosperity *1*."

With Mark and Hansen on board, we set out to fill in the rest of our presidential campaign staff and to give all employees of Friends of Herman Cain, Inc., corporate titles. Thus, I am the CEO, and among my closest key aides, Mark's title is COO and chief of Staff; Hansen's is executive vice president and deputy chief of staff; and Nathan Naidu, an eager, efficient, and well-informed twenty-five-year-old graduate of the University of Alabama who majored in political science, is assistant to the COO.

As of now, Friends of Herman Cain, Inc., has fifty or more staff members—the list is growing every day—as well as an impressive group of field operators and volunteers.

One of the defining moments of my campaign came in late February 2010, when I spoke at one of those summits, held in

Wisconsin Dells. I came out on the stage wearing a cowboy hat, took it off, and placed it on the podium. Then I gave my speech, concluding with the words, "I wanted to let President Obama know that in 2012, there will be a new sheriff in town." Then I put the hat back on and the crowd went wild.

When Hansen escorted me off the stage, she asked me, "Is this an announcement?"

"I just threw it out there," I told her. "Now let's see what happens." Then I went back to Atlanta. A few days later, Mark called and said, "Mr. Cain, I'm getting all these questions. What were you *thinking*?"

Two and a half weeks later, on March 20, 2010, Mark and Hansen flew to Las Vegas to join me for a strategy session at the Capital Grille Steakhouse, the place where the tables only went up to number 43. Working backward from November 2012, we laid out what would be required if I were really considering running.

At one point, as Mark was speaking, Hansen got up from the table, moved around the corner, and *prayed*. Then, when she rejoined us, we discussed how to make my candidacy happen, how we thought it could evolve.

Mark had actually discussed the presidency with me back in 2006. But then my cancer was diagnosed and everything went on hold as I underwent treatment. Now, four years later, in March 2010, I was cancer free and the time seemed right to revisit the possibility of seeking the presidential nomination.

Since that time, the Tea Party movement had happened—it really exploded across America on April 15, 2009—and as a result of all of Mark's activity with it, and with Americans for

Prosperity, he was able to establish contacts in most of the fifty states and to put on a Tea Party rally in Madison, Wisconsin. We were expecting two thousand people but eight thousand showed up.

We realized then and there that this Tea Party thing is much deeper than anyone had imagined. And I was one of the few potential candidates—maybe the only one—who realized what was happening in America because I was living it, so I could feel it.

By March 20, 2010, we all knew that the moment had come for our campaign to move forward. The first step would be for Mark and Hansen to create a buzz around me. They secured an invitation for me to speak in April at the Republican Leadership Conference in New Orleans.

At the end of the speech, I headed offstage, with the crowd on their feet and cheering. I walked back to the podium and said, "I just want you to know that there may be a dark-horse candidate running for president." The three thousand delegates went wild, and I felt like I was a rock star.

After New Orleans, we asked ourselves: What do we do in the June-to-November time-frame? We decided that I would travel the country, campaigning for Republican congressional candidates and speaking at Tea Party rallies and other large events so as to determine whether I would be acceptable as a candidate to grassroots Americans.

We soon found out: We did an event in Dayton, Ohio, and four thousand people came out to hear what I had to say—we called it our "watering the desert" effort. Then the results of the November 2010 elections vindicated what we felt was happening. We had planned for certain business and public relations reasons to launch our exploratory committee in April or May of 2011, but we now realized that support for my candidacy was growing, so we went ahead and pulled the trigger in January.

We were supposed to make the exploratory committee announcement in Atlanta, but while we were at a meeting in Phoenix, we found out that a snowstorm had closed the airport in Atlanta. So I ended up doing what turned out to be an almost nonstop series of interviews from Phoenix, garnering considerable nationwide attention.

Another major tipping point in my campaign came when I spoke to four thousand people at the 2010 Right Nation conference in Chicago. It happened that Glenn Beck was also a participant, and he asked me to meet him in his suite overlooking the conference.

I did, and Glenn said, "Mr. Cain, people have been asking me if I know who the next president is going to be. Now I can tell them I've met him."

I can tell you that that was a pretty big moment. It was nothing short of inspirational.

We were going along like gangbusters. Then in April 2011, a series of events occurred within mere days of one another—a period we would come to refer to as "Hell Week"—that nearly derailed my campaign.

I was scheduled to speak at a conference in Harrisburg, Pennsylvania, the opening event of a week that would take me to several cities around the country. We had been promised the use of a private aircraft. But on the afternoon before I was to head for Harrisburg, we were told that the private jet was no longer available.

At about five o'clock that afternoon, Mark Block and my advance man came into my office, each man looking as if he had just lost his pet puppy dog. It turned out that they were depressed because there was no Plan B. Mark then explained that the person who had promised us the plane shared it with his business partner, and that the partner had pulled the plug on our use of it.

I sat and thought for a few minutes. And then I said to Mark, "You're a good public speaker, so you're going to substitute for me in Harrisburg." Then I asked my executive assistant to put him on a flight and to book me on a commercial flight to San Jose, California, where I had a speaking date the next day.

Then I flew to San Jose via Dallas, where I had a brief stopover. As I sat on the plane, I didn't talk; I didn't read; I just prayed the whole time. When I arrived in Dallas, while I was sitting near the gate, a UPS pilot who was also traveling to California recognized me and came over to talk. When we got on the plane to San Jose, I was in seat 3B, while he was seated in row five, on the aisle, and I noticed that he was reading a campaign booklet I had given him in Dallas.

The man next to the UPS pilot asked him, "Do you know Herman Cain?"

"Yes," the pilot said. "He's sitting in row three."

The man came over, tapped me on the shoulder, and said, "Mr. Cain, I'm sorry to bother you, but how much money can I give and where do I send it?"

"You can give $2,500," I replied.

"You are going to get a check from me and my wife, and

I'm going to help you raise more money in California, where I have a business," he said.

When I landed in San Jose, the driver who was supposed to meet me in the baggage claim area was late, and I just made it on time to address eight hundred people at a home-school convention.

My next stop was Jefferson City, Missouri, for a Tea Party rally on the steps of the State Capitol Building. Mark, who had engaged in a dialogue about me with my good friend Colin Hanna, who had been asked to introduce me in Harrisburg, joined me in Jefferson City. Mark's presentation in Harrisburg had apparently been quite effective because at dialogue's end, I won a delegate straw poll—and I wasn't even there!

It was after Mark joined me in Jefferson City that our next problem surfaced: how to get to Fargo, North Dakota, where I was to address a dinner event. Mark called the dinner's organizer and when he said that he would send a private plane, Mark and I both said, "Thank you, Lord."

That was the *good* news. The private plane arrived all right, but it was no bigger than a crop duster and we had assumed that they'd be sending a jet to pick us up. I guess we were naïve. As there was only one pilot on board, I took the copilot's seat and Mark spent the flight hunched down in the tiny seat directly behind the pilot's.

On boarding that aircraft at two o'clock in the afternoon, we were told that we'd have a four-hour flight. That would give me just enough to time check into the hotel, freshen up, and change clothes. There was a problem, however. I had to do two radio interviews, starting at five o'clock. As the time for my interviews approached, Mark asked the pilot to land at the nearest airport. He set the plane down in northern Minnesota and I did the interviews from the flight-operations office.

We then went on to Fargo, rushed to the hotel to change, and arrived at the meeting room as the attendees were eating dinner. When they saw me, they stopped eating and gave me a standing ovation. It made me forget all about the flight to get there.

From North Dakota, we flew to Michigan, where I made two appearances: First I participated in a Skype presentation from my hotel room to a meeting near Tucson, Arizona, of the SaddleBrooke Republican Club, and the following day I spoke at a Tea Party rally on the steps of the State Capitol Building in Lansing.

Finally, after a week of close calls, we flew from Detroit to Atlanta. When we looked at our boarding passes, we discovered that we were on Delta 1045—there's that number again! That's the way God works.

Earlier on, Mark and I had agreed that if only we could get through Hell Week, we could then prepare for the first debate, in Greenville, South Carolina. For a while the decision to participate was touch and go, because funds we had anticipated receiving from some people in Texas and allocating to pay the $25,000 entry fee hadn't come in, as promised.

I ended up putting in some of my own money as seed funds because there were some positive signs, among them that I had won several straw polls, including the one held in Iowa at the Conservative Values Conference. And we had just been listed for the first time in a Gallup Poll, achieving the highest positive intensity score over the other declared and presumed candidates. This score measures each candidate's capability of generating enthusiasm among those Republicans who are familiar with the candidates.

Good things were happening, and I told my staff that we needed to "double down" so that we could participate in the debate. An accountant would never have made that decision; only an entrepreneur could have. I just had a really good feeling about it.

We got to Greenville at three o'clock on the day before the debate. I did the Cavuto show at four and then the team went out to dinner. Then I got to bed early, but not before calling Scott Bieniek, my campaign's general counsel, asking him to call my executive assistant, Lisa Reichert, with a special message from me not to worry about the office, but to come to the debate.

Lisa thought that was a wonderful invitation, so, as she told me after the debate, since she didn't have to go to the office that day, she decided to go by her church, the Stockbridge First United Methodist, and pray. It was the sixtieth observance of our country's National Day of Prayer. When she walked into the sanctuary around noontime, it was empty. That was unusual, and Lisa was able to go to the prayer rail and get on her knees for about twenty minutes and talk to God about all the things that were in her heart.

One of Lisa's prayers was for me: "Lord, you have already given him the words to say; now let everybody hear what he has to say."

When her prayers were completed, as she wiped her tears

from the prayer rail, Lisa looked down on the altar and saw that someone who had been there before her had left a prayer card with my name on it. As Lisa told me, "I knew that God was surely with you." Obviously her prayers were answered, because my words were heard by so many around the country.

The next morning I did a few interviews and relaxed. In the afternoon I took a nap and then had a bowl of soup before going over to the Peace Center.

In the green room, I was straightening my tie, and I looked at Hansen and said, "You know, I can remember when I wanted to make $20,000 a year and I thought: If I could only make that annual salary, I would achieve my American dream. And now I am in a presidential debate!" Hansen and I looked at each other, both of us thinking, "Life is an adventure, isn't it?"

The debate began. During the first commercial break, Tim Pawlenty, a really nice man—he was standing next to me on the platform—said, "Herman, we don't have anything to do for a few minutes. Want to play tic-tac-toe?"

"I forgot how to play it," I said, because I knew he was joking.

After the debate, when I walked into the media room, it felt like a hundred cameras and microphones were being stuck in my face, like a swarm of bees, and as I walked around the room, the whole swarm followed me.

Then we went back to our hotel and Mark and the others who had accompanied me to Greenville joined me in my suite. Lo and behold, Fox was running the whole debate again, so we sat there, glued to the television set. It was like watching a football game we had just won, all over again.

Lisa didn't get home till after 2:00 A.M. but she still managed to be in the office by 8:00 A.M. She was exhilarated and shared her story with me about the prayer card. I took off my glasses and pulled out my handkerchief. It was truly a "God moment." The whole experience was thrilling, the turning point that saved my campaign. I was inspired anew.

I continue to be inspired by the citizens' Tea Party movement. I'm inspired by other people I've met who are encouraging me to go forward in my venture. But, most important, I'm inspired by God Almighty. I feel compelled to do this and I'm inspired by all those little faces out there. And if you don't believe me, ask any parent or grandparent, because it's not about *us*, folks, it's about *them*.

We've got to save the savable and take back this country. I know now that I'm going to save my aunt Bessie and she's got hope. It's not about us. It's about our children and grandchildren.

As I travel around the country and am introduced at an event, I prefer a short introduction to a long one, because what I've done in the past is not as important as what I'm *going* to do.

I'm constantly trying to reach audiences based upon the reaction I get from certain things and then incorporate in my speeches. It's a dynamic process. It's not just a stump speech I'm giving.

I've used a written speech only once in over twenty years and it was the worst one I've ever made, so I said, "I'll never do that again." There will be times that I might have to use a script, especially when it comes to foreign policy and foreign relations, because I don't want to mess up somebody's name or title—you've got to be really careful not to misstate something when you are talking about leaders of other countries. But other than that, I just speak from the head and from the heart.

And what I say must be striking a chord, because I invariably get a standing ovation. In fact, if I *don't* get one, I'm sure I didn't give a good speech. Actually, there *was* one time that I didn't get a standing ovation and I thought, "It's because I didn't give a good speech." Well, I had—I was told it was a great speech—but the reason I didn't receive a standing ovation was that I was speaking at an accountants' convention. They're trained to be unemotional, so they sat there and just applauded. But according to their written feedback, they *loved* it!

Everywhere I campaign these days, people come up to me and ask, "Can you really win in 2012?"

"Well," I tell them, "I wouldn't be doing what I'm doing now if I didn't think I could win. Losing is not in my DNA."

Will it be difficult to unseat the incumbent president? Yes. His ratings hover around 45 percent. When I'm told that they have dropped to an all-time low of 39 percent, I'm not happy. Do you know who that 39 percent is? It's the people who don't have a *clue* what the real issues are—all they hear is what he's reading off the teleprompter—and many times it's deceptive, misleading, and incomplete. So he will be able to carry a lot of the people who are not paying attention. That's why his approval rating stays low—that percent of people are not informed voters, which means that if he raises enough money and does enough slick commercials, he could pull it out. So that's what we're up against.

But here's the good news. Here's what encourages me: The people who were independent—who aren't staunch conservatives or staunch liberals—have awakened to the president's weaknesses. He's weak as a leader, his economic policies have failed, and he's been inconsistent on foreign policy.

And here's the other thing: the citizen's Tea Party movement that the mainstream media wants to go away is *not* going away. In fact, it's getting bigger and it's getting stronger. For instance, in May 2011, when I was campaigning down in Florida and spoke to a packed, actually oversubscribed, house in the Villages, a retirement community in the center of the state—when I saw the place, I wondered out loud: "Why do I keep failing at retirement?" A lady there told me that she had never come out for one of these events before.

According to a poll taken in Iowa around that time, I was leading there. I'm quick to remind people that polls are nice barometers, and we're not changing our strategy based upon what barometric reading we get in Iowa, but those polls tell us that we know what we're doing. And we can make it bigger.

So as the pool of Republican presidential candidates grows, I'm not worried about Mitt Romney; I'm not worried about Rick Perry; I'm not worried about any of the other folks that I'm running against, least of all Ron Paul, whose campaign sends one of its "Paulites" everywhere I show up. Clearly the intent is to agitate, not to educate.

They do that because they're threatened by me and have made a conscious effort to try to discredit me and bring me down by always bringing up the same issue: the Federal Reserve. They're trying to destroy me on the fact that I was once affiliated with that body, and they've generated a lot of animosity toward it, some of it warranted, some of it not warranted, based upon some things I've said about the Federal Reserve.

In doing so, however, they've stretched the truth, saying that I did not want the Federal Reserve to be audited. I have never said that. I have said: "I don't think you're going to find anything to audit on the Federal Reserve." But they want you to believe that Herman Cain doesn't want the Federal Reserve to be audited.

I get the same stupid question at almost every one of these events. I know it's a deliberate strategy. How can a person randomly show up at a hundred events and ask the same stupid question to try to nail me on the Federal Reserve? It's really becoming annoying more than anything else.

But I've got news for those Paulites: It's not going to work, because the American people are a lot smarter than they are. That's what I'm seeing round the country.

But there are stupid people out there—the people who are ruining this country, and I'm worried about *them*. So we've got to get enough *informed* people off the sofa, get them to get out and get active. I believe we've got those people out there.

And even though I don't have the name ID that the other candidates do yet, and I don't have the perceived amount of money that some of the other candidates have, we've got support on the ground, across the country, in every state, in the critical primary states, that most of the media aren't even aware of. As of the beginning of July I released my first campaign finance report, listing contributions totaling $2.46 million, with zero campaign debt. So it's a lot easier now, as a result of the debates and many media appearances, to get that name ID. It's already starting to happen.

Still, a lot of people don't want to take the time to become educated. They are educable, but it's difficult to do so because a lot of them watch Jon Stewart and Bill Maher.

The good news about the Jon Stewart show is that he does make people aware of some of the issues that are happening in the news. But he always does parodies on that; you're not sure where he stands, which is fine, as long as you know that that's what he's doing.

Jon Stewart is a comedian—his words, not mine—and I'm a conservative. He takes shots at me not because I'm black but because I'm a conservative, and I find it hilarious that he mocks me in the tone of Amos 'n' Andy and Stepin Fetchit.

Stewart adds the mocking, but the name calling is nothing new to me. When I was on the radio I began to keep a list of the names I was called because I am an American black conservative. So I just added Stewart's comments to that list. But as Mark Block would say, "At least Stewart's audience knows who Herman Cain is."

Mark is right. That audience will be able to discern whether I am a Stepin Fetchit or not. I refuse to get into this whole race card thing. I've been called "Oreo," "sellout," "Uncle Tom," and "shameless." These are only the names that are printable.

The color of one's skin has nothing to do with qualifications for public office. What is important is one's character and the content of one's ideas.

I can understand, as a black conservative whose campaign is gaining momentum, that liberals in the media and elsewhere are getting nervous about me. I guess that Jon Stewart is trying to be funny. I don't hold a grudge against him. He doesn't offend me, because I know who I am. I just look forward to the day when he has to call me "Mr. President." He can do it in an Amos 'n' Andy dialect.

As for whether I will get a significant share of the votes of black Americans, my gut tells me that I will, for the simple reason that the victim mindset is losing favor in the black community. It no longer works because black people realize that if they want to achieve something in this country they can't accomplish that under the victimization system. That's why blacks have awakened to the deceptions of the liberal leaders and the Democrat Party.

Now, as I continue to campaign around this exceptional nation we are fortunate to live in, and to vote freely in, I tell everybody I encounter, "Our Founding Fathers did their job. Now we have to be the Defending Fathers of this nation. We have to defend the Declaration of Independence and the Constitution of the United States of America. It doesn't need to be rewritten, it just needs to be *reread* and *enforced*. That's our job."

I said as much on July 4, 2011, the 235th birthday of our great nation, when I addressed a Tea Party celebration in sight of Independence Hall.

Then I flew up to Manchester, New Hampshire, to participate in America's pastime by throwing out the first ball in an evening game. While I looked good, it was a low ball.

Now, as I continue my campaign for the Republican Party's 2012 presidential nomination, I recall and paraphrase the words of the great American patriot Ronald Reagan, who summed it up best by saying: "We're now going down a road called socialism.

"You can't pass freedom on in the bloodstream, it must be fought for, and protected, or one day we will spend our sunset years telling our children and our grandchildren what it used to be like in the United States of America when men were free."

As I make my way through the uncertain political arena, one thing is certain: I'm not going to have *that* conversation with my grandkids. And I don't think you want to have that conversation with *your* grandkids either.

We have a choice on November 6, 2012; we can get back on the road to freedom, democracy, and a democratic republic.

And if you choose to get on the Herman Cain Train, just bear in mind one thing: God is blessing America, and because of His blessing, come November 2012, when all votes are counted, we will score a trifecta. Both houses of Congress will be under the leadership of the party that truly cares about the future of our great nation, and Gloria and I will be living in the People's House at 1600 Pennsylvania Avenue.

— 12 —

The Cain Administration: The First Ninety Days

His lord said unto him, Well done, good and faithful servant; thou hast been faithful over a few things, I will make thee ruler over many things: enter thou into the joy of thy Lord.

—Matthew 25:23

It's midafternoon on Monday, January 21, 2013. The last Inauguration Day Parade float has just passed the presidential reviewing stand. The stirring march music has stopped, and invitees to the evening's inaugural ball—yes, there will be only one—are enjoying some down time before dressing for the evening's festivities.

I've become America's forty-fifth president—there's that persistent number again. I was sworn in at high noon. Now I'm sitting at my desk in the Oval Office, because I've got a lot of work to do before I dress for this evening's festivities and I've just convened a meeting of my senior staff, one that will likely last most of the evening.

Thirty days after taking office, I plan to convene a summit meeting of the heads of state and also the leaders of the opposition parties of our trusted allies. Doing so will enable me to outline my views on foreign affairs, as well as to take the measure of the men and women with whom I will most closely work in resolving the tensions that are eroding our confidence.

Incidentally, I've been examining the workings of the White House, and I intend to change some of the ways in which the presidency functions. I will define the office of the president; the office will not define *me*. And despite my high regard for the professionalism of those assigned to protect me, I and *only* I will in—God forbid—moments of national emergency determine when, where, and how I can best perform my duties as chief executive, because I happen to believe that the people want to see their president working in the Oval Office. I believe that they are comforted and reassured by having him at the very center of presidential authority and responsibility.

In order to help Americans regain their self-confidence, it will be my responsibility as president to help them regain confidence in their governmental institutions. I do realize, of course, that under the separation of powers, I cannot directly influence the way the Congress operates, but I can and will restore trust in, and respect for, the executive branch.

Thus my appointees will be people whose professional lives reflect high ethical and moral values. They will be expected to act in a decorous manner at all times and to arrive at work each day realizing that they serve their fellow citizens, not their self-interest.

And from the most junior clerical person to my chief of staff, White House personnel will be expected to have a copy of the Constitution of the United States nearby.

I will not come to Washington to do the usual, anticipated, accepted things. Rather, paraphrasing the time-honored words of Abraham Lincoln, I will bring the nation a new birth of freedom, one that will be dedicated to the people who, together with me, will ensure that the American dream, one that patriots have pursued in good times and bad, will not perish from this earth.

As in every executive position I've ever undertaken, I will determine the parameters of my activities. And while I respect those who have served before me, I will not follow in their footsteps. I will create *new* footsteps.

I will reduce the number of protocol-oriented events that presidents are seemingly required to attend. At a time of deepening national crisis, I simply cannot afford to allocate valuable time to things that do not advance solutions to this nation's problems. That's why I have decided to sharply decrease the number of inaugural night balls. Instead, Mrs. Cain and I will host a series of celebratory occasions, and they will be spread out during my first months in office.

My guest lists for state dinners and other important occasions will be light on A list celebrities and heavy on normal Americans who work each day to restore our nation to greatness. And unlike the practice of certain previous administrations, there will be no "paying" guests staying in the Lincoln Bedroom.

Once each month I plan to invite small groups of average citizens to join me for dinner and conversation. As someone who will have to spend most of my working hours in Washington, these events will make it possible for me to take the nation's pulse on the pressing issues, as well as to stay connected to the people.

In the waning days of the campaign, I was becoming more and more exasperated at the very thought of the candidates' talking about problems and not solving them, and so I offered not words, but deeds, regarding the major crises facing the nation: moral and economic decline, out-of-control entitlement spending, lax national security, and muddled immigration policy, as well as the pressing problems engendered by the government's current operation of the taxation, Social Security, and Medicare systems. All of these stemmed from a deficiency of leadership in the Congress and in the White House.

So as soon as the nearly ten-week-long "transition" period began, I lost no time in assembling my cabinet, identifying and recruiting the most capable people I could find to join my team, which in corporate-speak, I prefer to view as my executive committee.

I chose the members of my cabinet/executive committee based upon each one's having a true understanding of my ideology, as well possessing the ability to resist shooting from the lip and to be ready to challenge the status quo. I never would have accepted anything less, because, as you know, I'm all about challenging the status quo.

Regarding other appointments, my criteria have been the same as for my executive committee and vice presidential running mate. In fact, during my campaign, when résumés came in from Washington, I was reluctant to even take a look at any of them because most of those people have been brainwashed into a particular mindset: Name ID and money—that's what they're worried about.

Given my well-honed instinct for identifying the right people to get the job done, I know that I have chosen wisely. And now I must apply my corporate executive skills as a communicator to empower the entire federal bureaucracy in support of the achievement of our goals and objectives.

In contrast to my predecessor, I am not a community organizer advocating radical social policy with which to manipulate whole segments of the population; I am a community *energizer* who emphasizes the necessity for individual self-motivation.

My most urgent need is to begin to get America's economy back on track, so I am wasting no time in implementing Phase One of my Domestic Cain Doctrine.

I'm also giving thought on this, my first day in office, to resolving America's health care crisis, by replacing "Obamacare" with "Caincare," which entails formulating a compassionate approach to providing the best possible diagnosis, treatment, and follow-up care for Americans of all ages.

While I can and will call upon highly qualified specialists for information and advice, I must summon my own experience and abilities as a well-tested corporate leader to confront and solve the myriad crises besetting the nation.

As I go about fulfilling my campaign promise of reversing the Obama administration's attack on the American dream, I am already finding strength by recollecting the maxim of my mentor, Dr. Benjamin May: "It is not a tragedy not to achieve one's goals; it is a tragedy not to have goals to achieve."

And as I continue to sit in the chair occupied by many of my predecessors, I'll give thought to reasserting America's preeminence among the nations of the world. In doing so, I'll send a message of unwavering support to America's true allies, as well as giving notice to those who threaten the American way of life—and, by extension, the values of freedom-loving people everywhere—that their totalitarian actions will not be tolerated on my watch.

My overriding goal—to make America whole again—is no pipe dream. In fact, it is eminently attainable. And that's because I have the will—the "fire in the belly"—that has been the motivating force of my journey through life so far.

And once my immediate aims are accomplished, I will never be short of new goals to reach as I guide this nation toward renewal and once again assuming its rightful place as "the shining city upon a hill."

"How will you do all this?" you may ask.

The short answer is that I'll do what I did when I put Burger King's Philadelphia region on the right track; I'll do what I did when I helped restore Godfather's Pizza, Inc., to profitability; I'll do what I did during my presidential campaign when I defied the nay-sayers, not to mention the odds against me, and came out ahead of the field.

If you're looking for particulars, I won't lean on so-called wise men, as other commanders in chief have done. I will listen to them, but they'll have to try really hard to persuade me. I'll draw my own conclusions.

As for administration style, it has never been my practice on taking over a new job to call in all the existing vice presidents and just do what they say that they want me to do. I would treat our economic system as I would a corporation on the verge of bankruptcy: Step one, just make a 10 percent across-the-board cut from everybody and write me the plan.

Step two, we're going to do some vertical deep dives. We're going to look within your organization. We want you to justify the cost. What we want you to do is ask about everything: "Is it still in the best interests of this country?"

When you systematically continue to do this over years and decades, you can get rid of the Social Security debt that we have accumulated, with a personal retirement account option.

I've been asked what criteria I apply in selecting Supreme Court justices. My answer is, invariably: "I have three criteria: conservative, conservative, conservative. All I've got to ask them is: "Are you going to enforce the Constitution to the best of your ability?" That's *conservative*. And it's easy to figure out whether they're conservative or not, because usually they come off the district court bench, and you can go back and review the things that they have said and done.

I'm often asked: Would you reach out to people who have not been on the bench? And my answer is, "Oh, yes!" But that will be a lot harder to do.

What about my speech-making style?

I'm not changing a thing. I'll use a teleprompter, but only to make sure I get the names right. Reading it word for word and having a straight script would distract from interjecting some emotion.

I've also been asked, "What about the first lady? Will she be in the mold of Nancy Reagan or Hillary Clinton or Michelle Obama?"

My answer is "None of the above." Gloria wants to come up with a "Grandmommy Project," something to do with the children. As she has told me, "I don't know what it's going to be but it will be something relative to grandkids," which has been one of my themes. She loves those grandkids—we both do.

Well, it's now late afternoon—time to join Gloria and the rest of the family up in the family quarters for some down time before this evening's gala ball.

As I stroll out of the West Wing, I'm thinking about the awesome responsibilities I have undertaken at noon on Capitol Hill, and I'm thinking about the young woman who came up to me one day at a campaign rally and said, "Mr. Cain, when you become president, remember the people who are suffering."

So how can I help those people who are on the bottom of the economy? The best way to help these folk is not to take away the resources of the people at the top of the economy. I believe that truly helping those who are suffering as a result of the misguided economic policies of the Obama administration does not involve another handout program or another entitlement program.

If we can get the economy moving in the right direction, as I have outlined in my proposals and articulated in my "Economic Vision: Jobs for America" plan, we will move people up from the bottom. As my good friend, the late Jack Kemp, used to say, "A rising tide lifts all boats."

I'm also pondering the tremendous weight the presidency places on one's shoulders. I embarked on my journey to the White House because I knew that my personal and professional experiences would allow me to make a difference for the American people.

I'm not thinking now about the power inherent in the office of president just for power's sake. I'm thinking about how that power can be used on the people's behalf. I have come to the presidency to bring to bear the skills gleaned through a lifetime of hard work to inspire my fellow citizens to work with me in bringing America back to its rightful place of honor and preeminence among the world's nations.

As a man made exceptional by God's grace, I prayerfully look forward to beginning to make America exceptional again.

Well, I'm just about at the elevator up to the family quarters.

But bear with me for just a minute more as I confirm who I *am*.

It's obvious: I'm the president of the United States of America!

APPENDIX A

The Major Issues of the Day, According to President Herman Cain

FOREIGN AFFAIRS

Afghanistan

Some people in the media believe that presidential candidates must have well-defined positions on every domestic and foreign affairs issue. Obviously, it is naïve to think that someone running for president must have an answer for everything. In fact, a real leader has the right *questions* for everything.

In the case of Afghanistan, for example, I do not have access to every piece of classified information. To be clear, I want to be out of Afghanistan as much as the next person. But I am not going to propose a half-baked plan just to pretend I know everything, based on having only half the information I would need to make the right decision.

I was very disappointed in President Obama's June 22, 2011, statement, in which he proposed an abrupt withdrawal of our troops. That could potentially compromise the legitimate gains we have made in Afghanistan, as well as embolden our enemy and endanger those troops who will remain.

In essence, his statement was a stark reminder that while one might campaign in poetry, one must govern in prose. His call for a "middle course" appears to be yet another example of this administration's foggy foreign policy. While all Americans hope and pray for a speedy, victorious resolution to the war in Afghanistan to prevent the continued loss of our national treasure—our men and women in uniform—how we define an honorable exit remains to be seen.

President Obama was correct on one point: It is time for nation-building at home and it is high time that the Afghan people take more responsibility in bringing more peace and stability to their own country. Unfortunately for him, more and more Americans are persuaded that the president does not have a clue how to accomplish these goals.

China

In April 2011, many Americans were stunned to learn—through a report of the International Monetary Fund—that if the differences in the exchange rates between the United States and China are factored out (purchasing power parity), China could surpass the United States in economic strength in less than five years!

Further, a number of economists have estimated that if China's gross domestic product (GDP) continues to grow at approximately 10 percent annually, while the United States'

GDP continues to grow at its anemic rate of 2.5 percent or less, China's GDP will be larger than ours in fifteen to twenty years.

Neither of these observations can sit well with those Americans who believe that losing our world economic dominance is not who we are. More important, China's economic dominance would represent a national security threat to our nation, and possibly, to the rest of the world.

Let's look at the facts: China has a billion more people than we do. They aspire to having greater military might than we do. And they currently hold over 25 percent of our national debt. They have a different view from ours on human rights and how to maintain peace in the world.

It would be naïve to think that China would not be tempted to flex its worldly might if it were to surpass us economically and militarily. It would be equally naïve to think that we could influence their actions on currency or on anything else with diplomacy or two verses of "Kumbaya."

Sadly, the appeasement of the Bush and Obama administrations has shown that this is not a winning policy. Instead, the Chinese have been given more time to talk while they buy time to pass us in economic prowess and military might. Our China strategy should be to outgrow them!

I have no doubt that we *can* outgrow them, but only with an aggressive leadership that's courageous enough to propose and implement new economic strategies. I can promise that I won't avoid doing what is right just because the job will be difficult. That's not in my DNA.

We need to outgrow China because the U.S.A. is not a loser

nation. We need a winner in the White House. It can and will happen in 2012. As I have often said, "When the people understand it, they will demand it."

DOMESTIC AFFAIRS

The Economy and My "Economic Vision"

In June 2011, I released my "Economic Vision: Jobs for America" plan at a meeting of business people at the NEXT Innovation Center in Greenville, South Carolina. In the plan I spelled out my three "Economic Guiding Principles":

1. **Production Drives the Economy.** I firmly believe that in order to spur economic growth, the federal government must ease the burdens of excessive taxation and regulation. We must cut both corporate and personal taxes, make these cuts permanent, and eliminate some current regulations whose compliance costs weaken job creators.

2. **Risk-Taking Drives Growth.** To provide increased access to capital and incentivize companies to invest in worker training programs, new equipment, and emerging technologies, we must eliminate taxes on capital gains and their dividends. The capital gains tax represents a wall between people with money and people with ideas. And people with ideas are the catalyst for new businesses and new job growth. This is particularly true in the very important technology sector, where experience shows that new technology investments are the largest beneficiaries of reductions in capital gains taxes.

3. **Measurements Must Be Dependable.** This involves sta-

bilizing the value of the dollar by dramatically reducing the national debt. A stabilized currency will help to eliminate the uncertainty that impedes business expansion and job creation.

I firmly believe that the implementation of my vision will advance the economy as well as act to cut the unemployment rate in half when fully implemented.

Education

In recent years, it has become obvious that significant reform is needed in the way we educate our children. I believe it is time to unbundle education, from the federal government down to the local level. A critical component of improving education in America is to decentralize the federal government's control over it. Children are best served when principals, teachers, and parents, in concert with local municipality leaders, school boards, and states, are involved in making the day-to-day decisions about how to most effectively operate an educational system.

Unbundling education means putting kids first. It means rewarding those teachers who enrich the lives of their students, and it means holding those accountable who do not. It means putting students' interests ahead of union interests. It means making those on the ground responsible for the teaching and learning that goes on in their communities. It means expanding school vouchers and charter schools. It means offering parents choices for their children's education.

Appendix A

Energy

You don't have to be a prophet to see that an energy crisis is looming. This is largely because we have shut down the development of the energy resources we have right here in the United States of America.

We are the OPEC of natural gas and coal, but we don't want to offend the environmentalists, who don't believe that we can develop these resources responsibly. They say this despite the fact that our dependence on foreign oil has increased from 20 percent in the early 1970s to more than 65 percent today.

While we are creating this self-induced energy crisis—and while we continue the moratorium on oil drilling in the Gulf of Mexico—China, Cuba, and the rest of the countries in the world who do not like us will suck up as much oil as they can before our so-called government leaders wake up.

Let's face it, wind and solar energy development will not bring us to energy independence. Even the Department of Energy's "Billion Ton Study" has shown that those two sources combined could at best provide only 5 percent of our total energy needs.

But if we were to maximize all of our other domestic energy resources, we could become energy independent. This would not only help to keep down the cost of gasoline and the cost of everything else we buy, but it would also boost our economy and create hundreds of thousands of new jobs. And most important, energy independence would keep us from being vulnerable to the current instability in the Middle East or the whims of OPEC.

Natural resources are there for a reason. Use them! That's why they are *natural*. The Arctic National Wildlife Refuge (ANWR) oil reserves off our own continental coasts, oil-shale areas in the western United States, and nuclear-power development can create a path to energy independence.

The area proposed for ANWR production comprises less than one percent of the refuge's 19 million acres and could yield billions and billions of barrels of recoverable oil. The technology is in place to safely extract natural gas from our enormous reserves of shale-oil deposits.

It's as if the answer to energy independence is close at hand but excessive regulations and environmental extremists who influence timid legislators are holding America hostage to foreign oil.

Our nation cannot continue to spend billions of dollars to buy something we can produce right here at home. It is time for us to stop making other countries rich at our expense. It is time for us to reject President Obama's reasoning when he gave Brazil $2 billion of U.S. taxpayer money for oil exploration and promised that country that we would be its best customer.

When I become president, America will become its own best customer! We will adopt a Drill Here, Drill Now strategy. We will set this as our bold goal: zero dependence on foreign oil.

Entitlements

In America, social programs were originally designed to provide a financial safety net. But as the years passed dependency on the government for the most vulnerable in society became an entitlement. Today, too many Americans have shifted their expectations from government assistance to entitlement.

That has resulted in sociological and economic damage. Simply put, ever-expanding social programs are compromising our current and future financial stability. Current projections indicate that Medicare will go bankrupt by 2017, while Social Security will bottom out by 2037. Some experts believe these programs' demise will arrive even sooner.

For the generations who have paid into Medicare and Social Security, the federal government's inevitable failure to pay them as they retire is tantamount to stealing. The federal government's out-of-control fiscal behavior has frightened these people, causing them to wonder what kind of country they will leave for their children and grandchildren. It is my contention that we must revamp our social and welfare programs, so that our nation's less fortunate can be offered a "hands-up" instead of a "handout." To accomplish this goal we must return to free-market-based solutions that empower our fellow Americans to take control of their professional and retirement futures.

It is essential that we modernize our Medicare and Social Security programs, which began in 1965 and 1935, respectively. What worked then will not work today. It will be my responsibility as president to work together with Congress to empower, in a new and productive manner, America's golden age population.

Excessive Governmental Regulation

The federal government has amassed incredible amounts of control over our lives through its ability to regulate everything from emissions to food to businesses. While some regulation is needed to protect American consumers and taxpayers, excessive regulation has driven up the price of the goods and services we need and want.

What's more, burdensome regulations are increasing at an alarming rate. In 2010 alone, Washington forced forty-three more major new regulations on us. It is estimated that complying with regulations costs around $1.75 trillion annually, which is twice as much as the revenue the federal government received in 2010 from individual income taxes.

Alleviating the burdens of cumbersome regulations would provide an immediate boost for our weakened economy. It would send a signal to businesses that the government intends to maintain conditions that allow them to thrive, rather than bogging them down with costs that inevitably are passed on to their customers.

I will work to create reasonable regulations that cut down on bureaucracy while helping businesses succeed.

Government Spending

I and my cabinet officers will make a determined effort to cut the out-of-control spending by the federal government. We simply cannot pass on to our children and grandchildren the massive debt caused by liberal policies. We cannot allow them to be stuck with the tab for the government takeover of health care, industry bailouts, and failed stimulus packages. Each generation of Americans should seek to leave behind a better and more prosperous nation for the next, not saddle them with debt from reckless spending.

Nothing should be off the table. My associates will be prepared to wield red pens, to make tough choices, and to learn to say "no." Every federal agency, every government program, and every single expenditure must be reviewed and, if necessary, revised. I will expect nothing less. Budgets will be shrunk by target percentages. The days when the American taxpayer was viewed by politicians and bureaucrats as a bottomless piggybank will be ended.

When I served in the corporate world and money was tight, I asked our employees to drastically cut back spending and they did. Serious but responsible belt-tightening can save businesses and save our country. But this can only occur when we change the current leaders for ones who have had to make and keep to a budget, who have been tested day in and day out in the crucible of the business world.

I am the one candidate with the experience and knowhow to bring the United States back from the economic abyss that lurks on the near horizon.

Health Care

You've seen that commercial where they have demagogued the issue with medi-scare and grandma is tossed off the bridge. If we don't fix this problem, it's going to be our grandkids in that wheelchair that they'll be throwing off the bridge.

President Obama and the liberals in Congress have dismantled the free-market health care system and replaced it with health care "deform." They have extended the tentacles of government and diminished patients' rights, all in the guise of making health care a "right" for all. They've also made it more difficult and expensive for doctors to practice medicine, including specialized practitioners who are desperately needed to save lives.

I have no doubt that the great majority of Americans agree that it is time to replace Obamacare with a patient-centered, free-market approach. They understand that it is imperative that we institute sweeping tort reform that will allow physicians to practice medicine without fear of frivolous lawsuits.

Looser pay laws would be a great start! And loosening the restrictions on health care savings accounts would help to empower Americans to save and invest their own money to expand their options for care.

I believe that we need to level the playing field by allowing the deductibility of health insurance premiums, regardless of whether they are purchased by the employer or the employee. That would shift ownership of one's health care back to where it belongs, with the individual. As your president, I will lead the charge to accomplish these goals.

Appendix A

Labor Unions

Early in 2011, I was in California for a private conference hosted by two very successful and prominent businessmen. As the attendees heard presentations and participated in discussions on issues of national interest, about one thousand union members, many of them from the Service Employees International Union (SEIU), gathered across the street from the conference site.

They chanted slogans expressing their objections to the idea that a group of fellow Americans would have the audacity to meet and talk about shared beliefs in limited government, the free-market system, and constitutional liberties. My fellow conferees and I wondered: Why would anyone object to a group of citizens meeting peacefully to discuss common concerns?

The obvious answer is that labor union leaders, and the left in general, are not interested in a free society where people can think and make decisions for themselves. These people want a country dominated by big government, with union domination of businesses and our workforce. We've already seen that as conservatives continue to make electoral gains, the liberals and unions are resorting to demonstrations and, in some instances, to violence to shut us up, to intimidate us from daring to think and have a different view of the world than they do.

Likewise, union members went ballistic when Governor Scott Walker of Wisconsin proposed a solution to his state's fiscal problems—one that did not involve the raising of taxes, an initiative that the unions had forced the then-Democratic-controlled legislature to do for many years.

The desire of unions to make unsustainable demands on local, state, and federal government, irrespective of the devastating impact, is totally illogical, not to mention showing a collective disregard for the taxpayer. The courage displayed by Governor Walker in representing the people paying his state's bill is being replicated elsewhere. For too long taxpayers have looked on as all the chairs at the negotiating table were arrayed at one side. Now the taxpayers are being represented on the other side of the table.

This type of "Big Brother" government thinking inherent in union aims is becoming increasingly outdated. That dog won't hunt. Liberal lunacy is not in our national DNA.

The Length of Legislation

One of Jon Stewart's laugh lines concerned my comment that I would not sign a bill that was longer than three pages. I would have expected that, as a comedian, Stewart would have recognized that I was telling a joke—a joke with a meaning.

My comment was an exaggeration, of course, to drive home a point. But there will be no more twenty-seven-hundred-page bills in the Cain administration. I want short, clean bills addressing the specific topic of the proposed legislation. I want to end the Washington habit of throwing everything but the kitchen sink into a bill. I'm also going to insist that for the sake of transparency, every piece of proposed legislation must come with an executive summary for the public to read, so that everyday Americans will be able to understand what is up for congressional consideration.

Muslims in the Cain Administration

When you interview people for a job, you look at their work record; you look at their résumé; and then you have a one-on-one personal interview. During that interview you are able to get a feeling for how committed they will be to the organization's mission.

In the case of my interviewing a potential senior official who is of the Muslim faith, I will want to know how committed that person is to the Constitution of the United States. I will want to make sure that anyone, of any religion, serving in my administration—who is, of course, serving the people of our nation—is committed to our Constitution.

National Security

As president, my primary duty will be to protect the American people. I must ensure that our military and our security agencies are strong, capable, and well managed. I must also end the politicization of our national security. This vital area of American government isn't about politics, it's about defending America.

While diplomacy is a critical tool in solving the complex security issues we face, it must never compromise military might. We must also recognize the real and present danger to our country's future posed by terrorist nations and organizations. We should never be deceived by terrorists, nor should we ever negotiate with them. And we must be firm in dealing with nations that sponsor terrorism.

My presidency shall support our military with the best training, equipment, technology, and infrastructure to keep them in a position to win. We must also provide our men and women in uniform—the treasure of our nation—our veterans, and their families with the benefits they deserve for their sacrifices on our behalf. These heroes have served us. We must never forget to serve them.

Social Security

We must fix the problem by restructuring Social Security. I do not believe that raising the retirement age, by itself, will solve the problem. I support a personal retirement account option in order to phase out the current system. We know that this works; it worked in Chile when it was done thirty years ago.

Another example of how this works is what happened in Galveston, Texas, which opted out of the Social Security system back in the 1970s. As a result of having an account with their money in it, people retire with a whole lot more money. I am certain that personal retirement accounts will eventually make the system solvent and will help us go from an entitlement society to an empowerment society. For when you allow people to have a personal retirement account—with safeguards to prevent abuse—you empower them. When you force them to stay on Social Security and don't fix the problem, you are forcing people to stay hooked on an entitlement program.

Tax Cuts

Liberals do not want taxpayers to discover that the right kind of tax cuts will actually help the economy and help put people back to work. Dr. Daniel Mitchell, an expert on tax reform and a senior fellow at the Cato Institute, has documented the positive impact of lower tax rates. Tax cuts increase tax revenues. This is contrary to liberal beliefs, because the facts do not support their distribution-of-income ideology.

I offer you two examples of Dr. Mitchell's analysis. When John F. Kennedy got taxes lowered during his short tenure as president, tax revenues increased by more than 60 percent during the 1960s. Then President Ronald Reagan's tax cuts generated more than a 50 percent increase in tax revenues during the 1980s.

I realize that Big Government advocates will scream that my tax proposals are "crimes against humanity." But, in reality, these cuts will prove to be an effective means of truly stimulating the economy.

In Obama's world, taxpayers are not looked on as customers; we are viewed as "sheeple" and we the sheeple are starving for leadership. As a man named John who attended one of my New Hampshire in-home meetings commented, "November 2012 will be the end of an error."

The Obama administration and the congressional Democrats have been focused on making government larger, more bureaucratic, and more intrusive in our lives. They did not listen to the American people, believing in a terrible, mistaken way that their agenda would revive the economy.

In 2012, Americans will demonstrate with their votes that this is the time for genuine change, for the adoption of new and productive measures that will truly stimulate the economy.

The Tea Party

The liberals have called Tea Partyers all kinds of names. For instance, Nancy Pelosi said that we are "Astroturf." Harry Reid said that we are "unpatriotic." Janeane Garofalo said that we are "red-necked tea baggers." And some of the other Democratic leaders in Congress call us "crazy."

I'm reminded of my grandfather, who, we thought, would go crazy when we would upset him during the summers we spent on his farm. When we said, "Pa, you're going crazy," he would reply, "I'm gonna *show* you some crazy."

And that's one of the messages I sent to the Democratic leaders in the House when they controlled it: "Yes, we're crazy—we're crazy about the Declaration of Independence; we're crazy about the Constitution; and we're crazy about the greatest country in the world, and we want to keep it that way."

So that's why I keep reminding like-minded Americans: Stay connected; stay involved; stay informed. One way to accomplish this is for people to actually read the nation's founding documents, and to read them *carefully*.

Appendix A

PRESIDENTIAL POLITICS

Barack Obama: A President in Denial

I was saddened, but not surprised, by the mainstream media's swooning over President Obama's 2011 State of the Union address. I was not surprised by the reaction of an appliance repair man who visited our home the next day to install some new equipment. He told me, "I had a hard time sleeping after listening to the president's speech."

"Why?" I asked.

"Because I didn't hear anything in the speech that made me feel that America is safer as a nation. And I didn't hear anything that suggested that Mr. Obama has any idea how to grow the economy."

I'm certain that millions of Americans share that repair man's views.

One could not be comforted by the fact that under this administration, the total amount of U.S. Treasury Securities held by foreign countries increased by 18.5 percent in 2010. Or that in the same year, total bankruptcy filings were up 14 percent, while the unemployment rate remained between 9.4 and 9.8 percent, with new jobless claims averaging about four hundred thousand per week.

Add to that the fact that in his 2010 State of the Union address, the president said that creating jobs would be a top priority. Well, the mainstream media notwithstanding, we know the fate of so many of Obama's promises. Like the appliance man, we will continue to have restless nights because of this administration's broken pledges and failed policies.

In a speech to the U.S. Chamber of Commerce in February 2011, the president urged business leaders to "get in the game" in support of their country by spending more cash. He wants businesses to ignore the real state of the economy by following the government's lead in spending irresponsibly.

That would not be good for the country! The last thing we need is more bankrupt companies on top of the three-million-plus businesses that filed for bankruptcy during the Obama administration. That would only add to the already staggering level of unemployment.

I am convinced that businesspeople are not going to follow the president off the proverbial cliff when doing what he asks makes no sense. At the same time that he was trying to seduce corporate America into spending money in a stalled economy, his proposed budget for Fiscal Year 2012 increased the amount on which payroll tax insurance is paid by businesses, from $7,000 to $15,000 per employee. That's a sneak-a-tax! We were not supposed to notice it since the increase will not be effective until 2014. Well, *we noticed.*

This president is in denial that many Americans see his policies as redistributing individuals' assets. He's in denial about what the American people really want. He mistakenly thinks that the American people want what *he* wants—a government-controlled, socialistic America.

In 2012, the American people will with their votes show Mr. Obama that his assessment is very wrong.

The Race Card

While I don't believe that Barack Obama used racial issues to get elected, I do believe that many of his supporters selectively use race to cover up some of his failures. Whenever President Obama is criticized over policy mistakes, his surrogates tend to play the race card, as if there's supposed to be something inherently morally wrong in such criticism.

When I was doing my Atlanta radio show, I used to get callers who would ask: "How can you dare to criticize Obama since he's black?" This kind of double standard has no place in America.

My Candidacy, Against the Odds

Some mainstream Republican pundits and, more interestingly, Democratic operatives, have criticized my candidacy. The pundits have attacked my lack of political office-holding experience, dismissing me as a radio talk show host who offers entertainment.

The Democrats attack me because in their view, and rightly so, I am Barack Obama's worst nightmare!

To anyone attempting to scout my "weaknesses," I list three more.

1. **I don't claim to know everything;**

2. **I don't pander to groups;**

3. **I am terrible at political correctness.**

Like any candidate or, for that matter, the sitting president, I will make some gaffes and occasionally stumble in interviews with the press.

On the other hand, my *strengths* include: identifying, framing, and solving problems; surrounding myself with good and great people; and giving inspiring speeches to engage the American people in my common sense solutions process.

Oh! I also like to smile, laugh, and have fun with people. I think people can handle those qualities in a presidential candidate.

I realize that the road to the nomination and the White House is long and difficult. I know that we will encounter many new challenges along the way. When one recognizes that I am up against the skeptics, the critics, the establishment, the Democrats, the liberals, including a liberal-leaning mainstream media, the need to raise significant funds, and a host of other candidates seeking the same objectives, my candidacy seems to go against the odds.

But then, that's been the story of my life and career. Maybe my middle name should have been David. He defeated a giant against the odds.

APPENDIX B

My Leadership History

2004–2011—Board of Directors, AGCO Corporation

2001–2011—Board of Directors, Hallmark Cards, Inc.

2001–2007—Board of Directors, Reader's Digest
Association

1992–2008—Board of Directors, Aquila Corp-UtiliCorp.

1999–2001—Vice Chairman, RetailDNA

1996–Present—Founder and CEO, T.H.E., Inc., a leadership consulting firm

1986–1996—President, Godfather's Pizza, Inc.

1996–1999—CEO and President, National Restaurant
Association

1995–2011—Board of Directors, Nabisco

1991–1999—Board of Directors, Super Valu, Inc.

1992–2011—Board of Directors, UtiliCorp. United, Inc.

1992–2011—Board of Directors, Whirlpool Corporation

1992–2000—Board of Directors, Greater Omaha Chamber of Commerce

1988–96—Chairman and CEO, Godfather's Pizza Inc.

1988–2000—Board of Directors, Edmondson Youth Outreach Program, Omaha, Nebraska

1995–97—Chairman of the Board, Federal Reserve Bank of Kansas City, Missouri (Tenth District)

1994–95—Chairman of the Board and President, National Restaurant Association

1986–88—President, Godfather's Pizza, Inc., as a subsidiary of the Pillsbury Company

1982–86—Vice President and Regional General Manager, Philadelphia Region, Burger King Corporation

1980–82—Vice President of Systems and Services, The Pillsbury Company

1979–80—Director of Management Information Systems, Consumer Products Division, the Pillsbury Company

1978–79—Director of Corporate Business Analysis, the Pillsbury Company

1977–78—Manager of Corporate Business Analysis, the Pillsbury Company

1973–77—Manager of Management Science, the Coca-Cola Company

1971–73—Supervisory Mathematician, Department of the Navy, U.S.A.

1967–71—Mathematician, Department of the Navy, U.S.A.

1966–67—President, Morehouse College Glee Club, Atlanta, Georgia

1962–63—President, Student Government Association, S.H. Archer High School, Atlanta, Georgia

APPENDIX C

My Awards and Honors

2008
College of Diplomats, National Restaurant Association

2006
National Black Republican Association Entrepreneur of the Year for Outstanding Leadership and Economic Achievement

2004
Honorary Doctorate in Computer Science, Purdue University

2000
Bennie Award, Morehouse College, Atlanta, Georgia
Ernest Royal Pioneer Award, Multi Cultural Foodservice & Hospitality Alliance

1999
Inductee, Hospitality Industry Hall of Fame
Tribute, NRN (Nation's Restaurant News)

Order of the Tower Award, University of Nebraska at Omaha

1998

Doctor of Commercial Science, Suffolk University, Boston, Massachusetts

Spirit of Enterprise Award, Association of Private Enterprise Education, Dallas, Texas

1996

Horatio Alger Award, Washington, D.C.

Carl A. Nelson Award, Omaha, Nebraska

Jr. Achievement of Lincoln, Special Recognition, Lincoln, Nebraska

National Association of Insurance Underwriters, Spirit of Independence Award, Washington, D.C.

National Association of Independent Business, Special Recognition, Lincoln, Nebraska

Nestle U.S.A., inclusion in "Men of Courage II"

Nation's Restaurant News, Hall of Fame, New York, New York

Penn State University, Conti Professor, University Park, Pennsylvania

Member, The National Commission on Economic Growth and Tax Reform, Washington, D.C.

1995

Inductee, Hospitality Hall of Fame, Omaha, Nebraska

Distinguished Visiting Professor, Johnson & Wales University, Providence, Rhode Island

Certificate of Thanks, Nebraskans for Quality Health Care, Lincoln, Nebraska

Resolution of Gratitude, Creighton University Board of Directors, Omaha, Nebraska

Freedom Fighter Award, Lancaster County Republican Party, Lincoln, Nebraska

Omaha Small Business Network, Inc., Premier Fast Track Entrepreneurial Training Program, Omaha, Nebraska

Distinguished Service Award, Missouri Restaurant Association, Kansas City, Missouri

Dr. Geil M. Browning Award, Career Excellence & Community Involvement, Omaha, Nebraska

Certificate of Distinguished Service, Nebraska Restaurant Association, Lincoln, Nebraska

Sincere Appreciation as President of NRA, New Mexico Restaurant Association, Albuquerque, New Mexico

African American Award, Corporate and Community Leader, The Western Heritage Museum "Profiles of Power," Omaha, Nebraska

(50 influential people in the restaurant industry), Nation's Restaurant News

Special Recognition, Ak-Sar-Ben Court of Honor, Business & Industry, Omaha, Nebraska

1994
Omahan of the Year Award, Rotary Club of Omaha-Suburban, Omaha, Nebraska

Jefferson Award, American Institute for Public Service, KETV, Omaha, Nebraska

Humanitarian Award, National Conference of Christians and Jews, Omaha, Nebraska

1993

Distinguished Guest Lecturer, Cornell University, The Hotel School, Ithaca, New York

Distinguished Lecturer, Kansas State University, College of Business Administration, Manhattan, Kansas

1992

Foodservice Management Professional, Educational Foundation, National Restaurant Association, Chicago, Illinois

Advisory Board, People's Natural Gas, Omaha, Nebraska

Recognition Award, Minority Business Development Council, Dallas/Fort Worth, Texas

Special Recognition, National Black MBA Assoc., Inc., St. Louis, Missouri

Special Recognition, DECCA-Central High School, Omaha, Nebraska

Special Recognition, MUFSO, Dallas, Texas

1991

Food Service Operator of the Year-Gold Plate Award, International Food Manufacturers Association (IFMA), Chicago, Illinois

Outstanding Contribution, Sixth Nebraska Conference on Productivity and Enterprise, Lincoln, Nebraska

Gold Plate Award, IFMA, Chicago, Illinois

Certificate of Lifetime Membership, NAACP-Omaha Chapter, Omaha, Nebraska

Nebraska Small Business Associate of the Year, U.S. Small Business, Omaha, Nebraska

Special Recognition, Morton Jr. High School, Omaha, Nebraska

Outstanding Contribution, Value Diversity Television Broadcast, Marriott Corporation and Marriott Family Foundation, Philadelphia, Pennsylvania

Distinguished Service Award, All High School 20 Reunion (1971), Omaha, Nebraska

1990

Black Achiever in Business and Industry Award, North YMCA, Omaha, Nebraska

Entrepreneur of the Year, University of Nebraska-Lincoln, College of Business Administration

The Business Excellence Achievement Award, University of Nebraska-Lincoln, College of Business Administration

Outstanding Achievement & Leadership, Black DP Associates of Indianapolis, Indianapolis, Indiana

1989

Special Recognition, MUFSO, Nation's Restaurant News, New Orleans, Louisiana

Booker T. Washington Symbol of Service Award, National Business League, Birmingham, Alabama

High Business Achievements and Excellence, Civic Service, Frontiers, Inc., Omaha, Nebraska

1988

Honors, Nebraska Black Manager's Association, Omaha, Nebraska

Professional Achievement Award, Morehouse College National Alumni Association, Atlanta, Georgia

Life Member Society, The Urban League of Nebraska, Omaha, Nebraska

National Prominence Award, The Urban League of Nebraska, Omaha, Nebraska

1987

MUFSO Golden Chain Award, Nation's Restaurant News, Los Angeles, California

1986

High Achievement Award, Hospitality Management Program, Bethune Cookman College, Daytona Beach, Florida

Symbol of Excellence, Pillsbury Corporation, Minneapolis, Minnesota

APPENDIX D

CPAC 2010 Speech

Herman Cain: Good morning. Good morning. I want to thank those of you that stayed out late and drank a lot and still got up to come to this presentation this morning. Because now you can tell those that slept in what they missed.

Our Founding Fathers said it better than any group of men in history when they said, "We hold these truths to be self-evident, that all men are created equal, that they are endowed by their Creator with certain unalienable Rights, that among these are Life, Liberty and the pursuit of Happiness." It didn't say a guarantee. And there's nowhere in the Constitution where it says that the federal government should establish a Department of Happy. It said, "the pursuit of Happiness." But you and I know that the pursuit of happiness in this nation as defined and conceived by our Founding Fathers is violently under attack. It is under attack from liberal proposals with this administration and this Congress that are designed to strip us of many of our liberties. That are designed to restrict our ability to pursue our definition of the American dream based upon each individual's aspirations, each individual's motivation and each individual's determination; not the dictate of the federal government. And so as we wrestle with beating back cap and trade, and tax and kill; as we wrestle with beating back employee no choice act; as we wrestle with beating back health care deform legislation. You see, if something is supposed to reform something it is supposed to make it better. Well there's absolutely nothing in that proposed legislation, either version, that makes anything better. It just makes everything worse, so you can't call it health care reform. Health care deform legislation. All of these attacks on the pursuit of happiness, but there is good news. There is good news. The voice of the people is being heard. That's why they've been put on the back burner. That is good news. But we're not done yet. We've got some more work to do. We won't be finished until they're moved from the back burner to out the back door. And we have an opportunity to do that in November 2010. Move them out the back door.

Now here's how we do it. It's really very simple. You see the Founding Fathers, they did their job. The Founding Fathers did their job. I did my radio show remotely last night from here, from D.C., and I had a caller and I was talking about the Mount Vernon statement that was signed two days ago by nearly one hundred leaders of conservative organizations from D.C. and all over the country, and I was praising the wisdom and the foresight of the Founding Fathers, and a guy actually called and said, "How can you admire and praise the Founding Fathers when many of them had slaves?" I said you don't understand. The wisdom and the foresight of the Founding Fathers was to set the bar high and not low. It didn't say

I will share it with people. But if your argument is illogical and no facts, I will cut you off. I don't like to waste people's time. I don't like to waste people's time. So another caller called one day and said, "Mr. Cain, I love your show. I love what you, what you stand for." And she said, "I have a," she said, "I have a question for you." I said, "What's that?" "Where are the defending fathers? The Founding Fathers did their job." And she made me stop and think. We must be the defending fathers of this nation. We are the defending fathers. And there are three things that we need to do in order to continue this momentum. In order to be able to do what the second part of the Declaration of Independence says. Too many people call up and say my vote doesn't count, can we really change things? And I have to remind my audience, and I remind people when I'm giving talks, if you read the Declaration of Independence don't stop at Life, Liberty, and the pursuit of Happiness. Keep reading. And if you keep reading, it says when any form of government becomes destructive of those ideals, it is the right of the people to alter or abolish it. We've got some altering and abolishing to do. Keep reading. People like to stop right there. Don't stop there. That's the most important part, is about our right to alter and abolish. And I would like to point one thing out. I recited that without a teleprompter. I'm just saying.

And as the defending fathers, all of us are part of this defending fathers movement. I don't care whether you call it the Tea Party movement, the 912 Intelligent Fingers Movement, all of the various organizations. That is the beauty of this movement. It has multiple arms. It has multiple arteries. I said that for the benefit of my doctor friends that are here this morning. Thank you. Yes. Docs for patients. Three things we need to do, quite simply, to make sure we can abolish the liberal control of Congress in November. And just like the Founding Fathers set the bar high, I believe we need to set the bar high and say we will change control of Congress in November, starting with the House of Representatives. Not that we are gonna reduce the majority. No, we've got to set the bar high and make it happen, and here are the three things that we need to do in order to bring it about.

First, stay connected. Stay connected. Every one of you in here is connected to an organization or an initiative or a movement. Stay connected. And one of the reasons that we are experiencing the success that we are experiencing is quite frankly because more people are getting connected. One of my responsibilities is to encourage other people to get connected. Not everybody should or could run for public office. Not everybody should lead an initiative. But everybody can do something, and because we have become more connected as a movement in the last year, that's why some members of Congress are hearing the voice of the people. Now, the president doesn't hear us yet. His administration, they do not hear us yet. Harry and Nancy, they ain't listening yet. But the good news is, the poor conservatives in Congress along with some moderates and independents, they are beginning to listen. They're beginning to listen. That's why all of these threatening proposals have been moved to the back burner and it is our job to get them out the back door. So we've got to stay connected. One of the, one of the great things that I felt so proud of a couple days ago when we signed the Mount Vernon statement and many, many of the people that participated are here today, is that all of these nearly one hundred organizations who for so long have operated in their individual silos, have gotten above the silos and they're looking across. And somebody made the statement, I don't remember who said it first, nothing unites a movement like a common enemy. And we have a common enemy. It's called the liberal attack on this nation. So stay connected.

Number two, stay involved and encourage your friends and neighbors, if they'll listen, to stay involved. Now you can't make people get involved, but whenever you hear the statement, I don't have time to pay any attention to that stuff, you say well, one day you gonna wake up, to paraphrase former president Ronald Reagan, you're gonna wake up one day and you're gonna be telling your grandchildren what freedom used to be like, because this is an, an environment. We're already telling them that. This is an environment where we can't sit back. Do you know, it used to be where we could elect people, send them to Washington, and they were statesmen and stateswomen, and they would do what was best for the nation and best for their constituency. That doesn't exist anymore. This is why they have to hear from us frequently, loudly, and forcefully in between elections. That's the different dynamic that we're having to deal with. And that's why we have pushed these things to the back burner. We gotta stay involved. And so when you have an opportunity to talk with or influence some of your family members. My, my son, he's thirty-two. My daughter's thirty-eight and I finally got them to pay attention. You know how I got their attention? I said now Dad is not a kajillionaire, but Mom and Dad are gonna be comfortable in our old age and if I don't spend it all, the government is trying to take your inheritance. It's amazing how that got their attention. They woke up the next day as conservatives and didn't know it. I said welcome to the American dream. Welcome. So stay involved and encourage others to get involved. And, as I tell folk, get off the sofa and get off your anchovies because America's under attack, but we can save it.

Number three, stay informed. Stay informed. Because if you don't stay informed and if you don't know your facts and if you don't know your history, you can be tempted to drink the liberal Kool-Aid without knowing it and there's a lot of liberal Kool-Aid out there. And in order to stay informed, you have to be aware of what I call the liberal tactics that they use all the time consistently, no matter which liberal is talking. And if you, if you recognize their tactics you will be able to counter their tactics with good information, good facts and reasonable logic. But sometimes some of these reporters that I see on TV, they are blindsided so quick they don't know how to react. You have to stay better informed because if you look in the liberal playbook, you will find their three primary tactics. They commit what I call liberal SIN, capital S, capital I, capital N. They commit their liberal SIN and watch this whenever you see a liberal being interviewed on TV. They call the radio show all the time, and sometimes when I know that it's one of my regular liberals, I will warn the audience. I'll say, now, we're gonna take Thomas but you all know what to look for. He's going to SIN.

S—whatever the topic, he's going to shift the subject. They

do it every time. I was talking to a liberal one night on my radio show. I'd said did you know that President Obama has allowed the national debt to increase over $3 trillion in one year versus George Bush allowing it to grow $4 trillion in eight years. Almost as much in one year as eight years under the Bush administration. So the liberal says, well George Bush got us into this war. I didn't ask you about the war. We're not talking about the war. We're talking about runaway, tsunami spending. But they like to shift the subject. Watch that. Listen for it. And then if you're in dialogue with them, then you can get them back on track. So they SIN. They shift the subject. They do it all the time.

Second, I—they ignore the facts. To paraphrase Jack Nicholson in that famous movie, liberals can't handle the facts. They hate the facts. When President Obama started trying to sell health care deform, he continued to use the number 46 million people are without health insurance. Now fortunately, some radio talk show hosts, some news, cable news outlets, and a lady by the name of Sally Pikes of the Pacific Research Institute and others took a look at the data and unraveled that 46 million and found that it was not 46 million people who were going without health insurance because they couldn't afford it. Some of those people made enough money to buy it but they chose not to and some of those people that were counted in that number were residents of the United States of America but they were not citizens. And do we owe health insurance to every other person in the world? So when you start to peel back the numbers, it's not 46 million. And then in the president's address to Joint Members of Congress on just health care, he started using the number over 30 million. The real number's about 10 million. He still has a few others in there. And here's one other thing about health care deform that I want to make sure that I state in case somebody else didn't state it. We do not have a health care crisis in America. We have a health care cost crisis in America, and that proposal is not the way to fix it. I get the liberals who will call up and say, "Well what do you have against all Americans getting health care?" I said I have nothing against all Americans having health care. There is a right way and a wrong way, and unfortunately your party, your leaders, are trying to shove it down our throats, and we the people are saying not this time. You're not gonna shove it down our throats. So this is why we have to know our facts. Know the logic. Know the facts.

There are three things we need to do to bring down the cost of health care in America. This is not a health care seminar, but I gotta take advantage of this opportunity. So when, so when you are in dialogue with a reasonable liberal you can point out to them—I know, there aren't many of them, but you might get lucky and run across one on the bus or something. Three things would dramatically change the health care cost equation dynamics in this country. Number one, tort reform. Number two, level the playing field in terms of who you, who gets a deduction if you buy health insurance. Right now the employer gets a deduction but the employee doesn't get a deduction—and if you level the playing field such that it doesn't matter who pays for it, you get a tax deduction for your health insurance. Now let me just say parenthetically, we need to eliminate the stupid tax code. While we got it, we may as well do the right thing by the people. So that's number two. And then number three, allow insurance to be sold across state lines. If you do those three things, if you do those three things and if government gets out of the way, we won't have a health care cost problem. It's common sense. It's not rocket science. It's common sense. So know your facts, know your logic, stay informed. That's all we have to do in order to be the founding, the defending fathers.

The N, S-I-N—when they can't shift the subject on you, when they can't ignore the facts, they name call. You right-wing nutcases. You Tea Party—let me see if I can't remember some of them now. Nancy said we were Astroturf. Harry Reid said we were unpatriotic. Janeane Garofalo said that we were rednecked teabaggers. And some of the other Democratic leaders in Congress called us crazy. Well, it reminded me of my grandfather when we used to spend time on the farm during the summer. And when we did something to upset my grandfather, we thought he went crazy. And Grandpa's favorite phrase when he was coming after us, when we'd be saying, "But, Pa, you, you're going crazy." He would say, "I'm gonna show you some crazy." And that's one of our messages to the leaders in Congress. Yes we are crazy, we're crazy about the Declaration. We are crazy about the Constitution. And we are crazy about the greatest country in the world—and we want to keep it that way. Yes, we're crazy. We're crazy. Oh, yeah. We're crazy. Yeah, next time they say you all are a bunch of crazies say, "Thank you. Thank you." Yeah, we're crazy. We're crazy about this country. We're crazy about our children and our grandchildren. And so that's what we have to do as defending fathers. That's my message to you today. Stay connected, stay involved. Stay connected, stay involved and stay informed. And that way you can combat the liberal SIN.

And with the Winter Olympics going on, it reminded me of the closing song, the words to the closing song of the 2000 Olympics, that reminds each of us as defending fathers of our responsibility. The words to the closing song of the 2000 Olympics said, "Life can be a challenge. Life can seem impossible. It's never easy when there's so much on the line. But you can make a difference. There's a mission just for you. Just look inside and you will find just what you can do. The power of one begins with believing that you hold the key to all of your achieving. Just look inside and you will find just what you can do. The power of one begins with believing that you hold the key to all of your achieving." We have a message for the president, his administration, Harry and Nancy, and the liberals. We, the people, are still in charge of this country.

APPENDIX E

May 21, 2011, Speech

This is the speech that I delivered on May 21, 2011, at Centennial Olympic Park, in Atlanta, Georgia, when I announced my candidacy for the Republican Party's nomination for president of the United States:

Thank you. Love you. Love you. Love y'all. Aw, shuckyducky, as the man would say. I've got to tell you, let me. Thank you. I see some Antioch (church) people back there, a few of them back there, yelling. I understand that my aunt Bessie is here. Oh, there she is. Now do you know why it is so momentous that my aunt Bessie is here? She hasn't decided if she can vote for me yet. But I'm going to change her mind today. That's right; we are going to change the minds of a lot of folk in America.

I want to thank all of you again from the absolute bottom of my heart for your being here because there were some skeptics, you know, who didn't think anybody would show up for an announcement from me. And the last time I heard, there were fifteen thousand of you all right here.

Thank you. Thank you. You know it has been this kind of

encouragement that has gotten me to this point. And it is this kind of encouragement that I believe is going to take us where we are trying to get to.

You know, many of you know that I grew up right here in Atlanta, Georgia. Right here in Atlanta, Georgia. I stand in the shadows of my upbringing. I stand here today as the son of a chauffeur and a domestic worker who taught me and my brother three of the most important values we could have ever learned: belief in God, belief in what we could do for ourselves, and belief in this exceptional nation called the United States of America.

Believe in it. You know that the people who are struggling the most are the ones that don't believe in this nation. They don't believe in the values of this nation. My parents never uttered the word "victim" because they never felt like victims, having an opportunity to be in this nation despite its challenges.

So I stand here today as Luther and Lenora's oldest son, in my hometown. I stand here today in this hour, in the shadow of the Olympic flame, which represents not only the determination of those that go to the Olympics every four years with their own determination, but it also signifies the great spirit of this great country, the spirit of America. That's what it signifies.

And it is this spirit of America and the determination of America and the determination of its people that we are going to take our country back. We're going to take it back. This day, this hour, the spirit of America and the spirit of the Olympics here in this park. When people participate in the Olympics every four years, they don't go to the Olympics to come in second. They go to the Olympics to win.

And you see, just like the spirit of the Olympics, number two is not in America's DNA. We don't do number two. Right here, this day, this hour, this moment. Right here, this day, this hour, this moment I have looked inside myself and at this moment, this day amongst thousands and thousands of my friends, and with my family here with me, and associates that I have known throughout the years.

This day, this hour, this moment, I came here to declare my candidacy for the Republican nomination for president of the United States of America. This moment. This moment.

And just to be clear, in case you accidentally listened to a skeptic or Doubting Thomas out there, just to be clear, let me say it again: I'm running for president of the United States. And I'm not running for second. I'm not running for second; I'm running for number one.

Now let me tell you, because I've had reporters ask me sometimes: "Well, are you just running to get attention? And maybe come in second? Or maybe to get a cabinet position?"

I say, "You don't know very much about me. You don't run for second. I don't run for second. I'm running to be number one."

Now let me tell you some of the reasons I'm running for president of the United States. One of the biggest reasons is that we have become a nation of crisis. We have a moral crisis, we've got an economic crisis, we've got an entitlement spending crisis, we've got an immigration crisis, we've got a foggy foreign affairs crisis, and we've got a deficiency of leadership crisis in the White House.

There is a big difference between leadership and position-ship. A big difference between leadership and position-ship. Let's look at the facts relative to all of these crises. We have anemic economic growth. In the first quarter of this year our GDP only grew by 1.8 percent. That is anemic, especially when China is growing 10 percent compound. And if we don't increase our growth rate, they are going to be as big as we are in five years if you take out the differences in exchange rate.

If we allow China to become as economically powerful as we are, you know they are going to try to develop a military might as big as ours. And I don't know about you, but I'm not going to allow America to be number two in the economy, number two militarily on our watch. Not on our watch.

We are a nation of crises. Look at the facts, don't listen to the rhetoric. A 9 percent unemployment rate, with nearly 15 million people out of work. Forty-seven million people on food stamps, that's 14 million more than there were when the current occupant of the White House took over. Four dollars a gallon of gas and it's not over yet. One trillion dollars in spending to stimulate the economy and it didn't stimulate diddly.

All of that and now to have a $14 trillion national debt and the debate in Washington, D.C., is going on about: Do we raise the debt ceiling again? Let me tell you what the Cain Doctrine will be. We ain't raising the debt ceiling. We're going to cut the spending. It's called reduce. So look at the facts. Don't just listen to the rhetoric. Look at the facts. The stuff is not working.

It's not working. So, the only thing that I can conclude is: It's time to get real, folks. It's time to get real.

Hope and change ain't working. Hope and change is not a solution. Hope and change is not a job. Hope and change is not a new business. Hope and change is not a vision. We need a new vision in this country and that means we need a new person leading this nation in the White House. It ain't working.

Now I want to ask you a few questions. Is America ready for real results? Is America ready for common sense solutions? Is America ready to rekindle the spirit of America? And is America ready for a real leader, not a reader? Do you want a leader? Or do you want a reader?

I know it took some people a little time to connect the dots on that last statement, but they finally got it. Since you answered yes to those questions, let me describe our new vision. I don't call it my vision. My job as the leader is to define it, key it up, share it with you. It becomes our vision. Because you know what? I can't do this by myself. This will be our vision. Not a political vision, not the agenda of one person, but it has to be the agenda of the people of this country. I call it our vision.

In order for us to be able to achieve and make a reality out of our vision, we're going to need some new plans, set some new priorities, and certainly get some new people around the president, this new president, that are better than the ones we got to turn the vision.

Our new vision is real economic growth, not anemic growth, and in order to do it, we've got to lower tax rates for corporations and individuals. We've got to work on taxes for repatriated properties. We've got to take the capital gains tax to zero. We've got to give the workers of America a real payroll tax holiday and then put a bow around the first three and make the tax rates permanent. That would lead to economic growth.

Our vision includes a real energy independence plan. A real one. Not one that someone just reads off a teleprompter. One of the things that is so frustrating about it is that we have the resources to become energy independent, we simply need to pull the resources together in order to make it happen.

You know that I will never go to a foreign country, like Brazil, loan them money, and then tell them we are going to be their best customer—for their oil. Let me share with you another one of the Cain Doctrines. America is going to be its own best customer—for its own oil. Drill here! Drill now! Right here in the U.S.A. We will be our own best customer.

And as president of the United States, I want to make sure that we are our own best customer when it comes to our energy needs and our energy resources. It's not that we don't have the resources, we've just got too much bureaucracy that keeps getting in the way.

Our new vision means immigration through the front door and not through the back door or the side door. This nation was built on immigrants. Legal immigrants. And if we attack the right problem, actually we have four problems rather than one. We've got to secure the border, we've got to enforce the laws that are already in place, we've got to promote the path to citizenship that is in place. Why don't you ask the millions of people who have come here legally? They'll tell you about the path. And then the fourth thing that we have to do in order to deal with the nation's illegals that are already here is to realize that the federal government is not going to solve the problem. In our new vision we will empower the states to solve the problem of those who are here illegally. That's how we take care of that problem.

And the last thing that you will get from a Herman Cain presidency is suing a state because they are trying to protect themselves. We shouldn't be suing Arizona; we ought to send them a prize. A Peace Prize. Suing a state of the United States of America? That's a major disconnect.

I love it when the skeptics want to criticize me for "lack of foreign policy experience." Let me tell you what I know about foreign policy experience. I know that you don't throw your friends under the bus. That's what I know about foreign policy. You don't have to have years in the State Department to figure that out.

Know who your friends are. Know who your enemies are. And don't throw your friends under the bus. I was shocked last week when President Obama threw Israel under the bus.

Let me tell you what the Cain Doctrine will be relative to our friends. And I'll share with you later my doctrine relative to our enemies. I've got stuff for them too. But relative to Israel, we have had a relationship that most of us have appreciated for decades. In the Cain Doctrine the word would simply be: If you mess with Israel, you're messing with the United States of America. Don't mess with us. Don't mess with us. Is that real clear? That is what I mean by real clear foreign policy. Know who your friends are. Know who your enemies are.

And it's *our* new vision. It's not the establishment's. It's not the politicians'. Let me also say that over the years this nation has gradually slipped into an entitlement society. Well I've got to tell you folks, not only do I believe it is possible, but I also know that it is possible, that it is time to restructure rather than reshuffle programs. If we do this we can take this entitlement society to an empowerment society.

You know the Founding Fathers did their job. And they did a great job. They kept it simple. They wrote the Declaration of Independence; they designed the Constitution of the United States of America. And one of the things that is part of our new vision is that we don't need to rewrite the Declaration, we don't need to rewrite the Constitution of the United States. Rewrite it? We need to *reread* the Constitution and to enforce the Constitution. We don't need to rewrite. Let's reread.

I know that there are some people that are not going to do that. So here's a word for the benefit of those who don't want us to reread it because they don't want us to live by the Constitution. There's a little section in there that talks about Life, Liberty, and the Pursuit of Happiness. You know these ideals that we live by and believe in, your parents believed in. What they instilled in you is that you don't stop reading when you get to the part about Life, Liberty, and the Pursuit of Happiness. They said, don't stop there, keep reading. Because that's when the document says, "When any form of government becomes destructive of those ideals, it is the right of the people to alter or abolish it." We've got some altering and some abolishing to do.

In 2012, we are not only going to keep control of the House of Representatives, we are also going to control the United States Senate and take it back. And in 2012, we are also going to run the trifecta and alter the occupant of the White House with a new president.

And for sure, we are all going to have to work a little harder, we are all going to have to be a little smarter. I realize we are not going to convert everybody over to our conservative way of thinking. We're not going to sell everybody on our new vision with new leadership, new people, new ways to look at the issues. As a good friend of mine once told me, "All you can do is save the savable." And, you know, between now and November 2012, I think I'm going to save my aunt Bessie. I think she's got hope.

So we've got a lot of work to do, folks. But I believe we can do this. If I didn't believe we could do this, I wouldn't be doing it. So we've all got to do a little more. We've got to work a little bit harder in order to take back this country. It's going to be tough. I'm up for the fight. I'm up for the challenge. And I know that you are, too.

The Founding Fathers did their job. Now we have to do our job. We have to be the defending fathers. I've been blessed with two adult kids; they've grown and gone. We've got three grandkids. But it's not about us. And I know everybody here today shares this feeling. As I have traveled all over this country, talking to groups day in and day out, at town hall meetings, large rallies, small events, my message has been consistent, it's not about us. In my travels I have found that people are ready to do whatever it takes to take this nation back.

And I firmly believe in my heart that God is in this journey. That God is in this journey. And in November 2012, the day after the election, when we wake up that morning and all the votes are counted, and they declare not only all of the local election results, the statewide election results, the congressional results, the senatorial results, and when we wake up and they declare the presidential results, and Herman Cain has been elected, we'll be able to say: "Free at last, free at last, thank God almighty this nation is free at last again."

Thank you, ladies and gentlemen. God bless you. God bless the U.S.A.

ACKNOWLEDGMENTS

To my wife, Gloria, for her unwavering support, patience, and sacrifice.

To Jerry and Deborah Strober, for their expert and professional assistance.

To all of my staff at THE New Voice, who worked hard to make this project a reality.